TEACHER'S PET PUBLICATIONS

LITPLAN TEACHER PACK

for

Witness

based on the book by
Karen Hesse

Written by
Christina Stone

TABLE OF CONTENTS

ABOUT THE AUTHOR

Karen Hesse

Karen Hesse is originally from Baltimore, Maryland. While growing up, she spent a lot of time at her local library, where a friendly librarian supplied her with a healthy dose of children's books to occupy her time at home. She fell in love with Dr. Seuss' use of language and read constantly. While in elementary school, Hesse received encouraging compliments from her teachers who admired her creativity in writing.

Her teachers' compliments combined with her passion for reading encouraged her to become the person she is today. "One day, when I was eleven, I wandered out of the children's section of the library and got my hands on John Hersey's *Hiroshima*. Here were people surviving under the most extreme adversity and behaving in a manner of extraordinary grace and dignity. I think you can hear the echo of *Hiroshima* in my work."

Hesse later graduated from the University of Maryland where she earned her B.A. in English with double minors in Psychology and Anthropology. After various odd jobs, she finally got the chance to follow her dream of becoming an author.

Hesse still loves writing and can't wait to get to her keyboard every morning. She also enjoys reading, hiking, traveling, and spending time with friends and family. She currently lives in Vermont with her husband and two teenage daughters.

Major Works
Hesse has written several children's books and young adult novels. Her most popular works include *Phoenix Rising, Letters from Rifka, The Music of Dolphins, Witness*, and *Out of the Dust.*

Awards
Out of the Dust won the 1998 Newberry Medal and the Scott O'Dell Award for Historical Fiction.

INTRODUCTION *Witness*

This LitPlan has been designed to develop students' reading, writing, thinking, and language skills through exercises and activities related to *Witness.* It includes twenty one lessons, supported by extra resource materials.

The **introductory lesson** introduces students to the title and themes of the book. This activity forces students to realize that the outward appearance of people/objects isn't always as important as what is inside. Following the introductory activity, students are given the materials they will be using during the unit. At the end of the lesson, students begin the pre-reading work for the first reading assignment.

The **reading assignments** are approximately thirty pages each; some are a little shorter while others are a little longer. Students have approximately 15 minutes of pre-reading work to do prior to each reading assignment. This pre-reading work involves reviewing the study questions for the assignment and doing some vocabulary work for selected vocabulary words they will encounter in their reading.

The **study guide questions** are fact-based questions; students can find the answers to these questions right in the text. These questions come in two formats: short answer or multiple choice. The best use of these materials is probably to use the short answer version of the questions as study guides for students (since answers will be more complete), and to use the multiple choice version for occasional quizzes.

The **vocabulary work** is intended to enrich students' vocabularies as well as to aid in the students' understanding of the book. Prior to each reading assignment, students will complete a two-part worksheet for selected vocabulary words in the upcoming reading assignment. Part I focuses on students' use of general knowledge and contextual clues by giving the sentence in which the word appears in the text. Students are then to write down what they think the words mean based on the words' usage. Part II nails down the definitions of the words by giving students dictionary definitions of the words and having students match the words to the correct definitions based on the words' contextual usage. Students should then have an understanding of the words when they meet them in the text.

After each reading assignment, students will go back and formulate answers for the study guide questions. Discussion of these questions serves as a **review** of the most important events and ideas presented in the reading assignments.

After students complete reading the work, there is a **vocabulary review** lesson which pulls together all of the fragmented vocabulary lists for the reading assignments and gives students a review of all of the words they have studied.

Following the vocabulary review, a lesson is devoted to the **extra discussion questions/writing assignments**. These questions focus on interpretation, critical analysis, and personal response, employing a variety of thinking skills and adding to the students' understanding of the novel.

There is a **hate crimes project** in this unit. This project requires students to research hate crimes against a specific group.

There are three **writing assignments** in this unit, each with the purpose of informing, persuading, or having students express personal opinions. The first writing assignment asks students to write from the perspective of someone in the 1920's time period. The second asks students to persuade someone to practice tolerance, and the third asks students to write about one of the many issues related to this book.

There is a non-fiction **reading assignment**. Students must read non-fiction articles, books, etc. to gather information about their themes in our world today.

The **review lesson** pulls together all of the aspects of the unit. The teacher is given four or five choices of activities or games to use which all serve the same basic function of reviewing all of the information presented in the unit.

The **unit test** comes in two formats: multiple choice or short answer. As a convenience, two different tests for each format have been included. There is also an advanced short answer unit test for advanced students.

There are additional **support materials** included with this unit. The **Unit Resource Materials** section includes suggestions for an in-class library, crossword and word search puzzles related to the novel, and extra worksheets. There is a list of **bulletin board ideas** which gives the teacher suggestions for bulletin boards to go along with this unit. In addition, there is a list of **extra class activities** the teacher could choose from to enhance the unit or as a substitution for an exercise the teacher might feel is inappropriate for his/her class. **Answer keys** are located directly after the **reproducible student materials** throughout the unit. The **Vocabulary Resource Materials** section includes similar worksheets and games to reinforce the vocabulary words.

The **level** of this unit can be varied depending upon the criteria on which the individual assignments are graded, the teacher's expectations of his/her students in class discussions, and the formats chosen for the study guides, quizzes and test. If teachers have other ideas/activities they wish to use, they can usually easily be inserted prior to the review lesson.

UNIT OBJECTIVES *Witness*

1. Students will demonstrate their understanding of the text on four levels: factual, interpretive, critical, and personal.
2. Students will make connections with the material in the text and apply the lessons learned to their lives.
3. Students will be given the opportunity to practice reading aloud and silently to improve their skills in each area.
4. Through reading the story *Witness*, students will compare hatred to tolerance in regards to the treatment of others.
5. Students will answer questions to demonstrate their knowledge and understanding of the main events and characters in *Witness* as they relate to the author's theme development.
6. Students will enrich their vocabularies and improve their understanding of the novel through the vocabulary lessons prepared for use in conjunction with the novel.
7. Students will demonstrate the ability to write effectively to inform by developing and organizing facts to convey information. Students will demonstrate the ability to write effectively to persuade by selecting and organizing relevant information, establishing an argumentative purpose, and by designing an appropriate strategy for an identified audience. Students will demonstrate the ability to write effectively to express personal ideas by selecting a form and its appropriate elements.
8. Students will read aloud, report, and participate in large and small group discussions to improve their public speaking and personal interaction skills.

READING ASSIGNMENTS *Witness*

Date Assigned	Assignment	Completion Date
	Assignment 1 Act 1	
	Assignment 2 Act 2	
	Assignment 3 Act 3	
	Assignment 4 Act 4	
	Assignment 5 Act 5	

UNIT OUTLINE *Witness*

1 Introduction Activity Project Assignment PV1	**2** Time Period Information & Background Knowledge	**3** Read Act 1	**4** Study ?s 1 Vocabulary 1 Character Cut Outs	**5** Nonfiction Assignment PV2
6 Read Act 2	**7** Study ?s 2 Vocabulary 2 Writing Assignment #1	**8** Speaker PV3	**9** Read Act 3 Oral Reading Evaluation	**10** Study ?s 3 Vocabulary 3 Hate Crimes in Depth
11 Writing Assignment #2 PV4	**12** Read Act 4	**13** Study ?s 4 Vocabular 4 PV5	**14** Read Act 5	**15** Study ?s 5 Vocabulary 5 Extra Discussion Questions
16 Extra Discussion Questions Cont.	**17** Writing Assignment #3	**18** Project Presentations Unit Reflection	**19** Vocabulary Review Letter to Author	**20** Unit Review
21 Unit Test				

Key: P = Preview Study Questions V = Vocabulary Work R = Read

STUDY GUIDE QUESTIONS

STUDY GUIDE QUESTIONS *Witness*

Assignment 1
<u>Act 1</u>

1. Why are several young girls in the town upset about Miss Harvey's decision regarding "The Fountain of Youth"?
2. Who is Willie Pettibone?
3. How does Leanora's mother die?
4. Aside from liking Leanora despite her race, what sets Esther Hirsh apart from the other speakers in the novel?
5. Why does Leanora walk out into the cold without a coat, hat, or shoes?
6. What does Sara Chickering do when Leanora shows up at her door in the freezing weather with no coat, hat, or shoes?
7. Iris Weaver owns her own restaurant but also has another, more secretive job. What is it?
8. How do Harvey and Viola Pettibone feel about the Ku Klux Klan?
9. What happens to Lewis, a boy from school?
10. What reason does Sara Chickering give for never marrying?

Assignment 2
<u>Act 2</u>

1. Who is Bobby Franks?
2. Why does Leanora help Mr. Field?
3. Where does Esther think her mother is?
4. Harvey Pettibone tells his wife about what Johnny Reeves was preaching in his store earlier that day. What does Johnny say about women and happiness?
5. What has Iris Weaver done with the money she has made smuggling in illegal alcohol?
6. Mr. Field offers Leanora gifts that she would love to have. Each time he offers her something she wants, she declines his offer. Why doesn't she take his gifts when she wants them so much?
7. Why does Merlin Van Tornhout get arrested?
8. When does the KKK set the cross on fire?
9. What groups does the KKK target?
10. Why does Ira Hirsh consider moving out of Sara Chickering's house?

Assignment 3
<u>Act 3</u>

1. What happens when Iris Weaver gets caught with illegal alcohol in her car?
2. What does the KKK do to keep up the appearance that they are serving the community?
3. Why does Esther stand on the railroad tracks and refuse to move as a train approaches?
4. Why is there an article about Leanora in the newspaper?
5. Leanora's father gets a threatening letter in the mail. What does it say?
6. What does the KKK have against Esther and her father?

7. The lawyer who is arguing Leopold and Loeb's trial is not arguing that they were innocent. He admits they were guilty. What is his argument instead?
8. What could Merlin Van Tornhout do to advance in the KKK?
9. What ends up happening to Leopold and Loeb, the two boys being tried for the murder of Bobby Franks?
10. Harvey puts brooms on sale for one penny and women stampede his store to get one. Twelve women are injured as a result and have to go to the doctor for medical attention. Viola says the doctor might just charge Harvey for the medical bills, since he hasn't been too happy with him lately. What does Harvey say will happen if the doctor unfairly tries to charge him for the medical bills?
11. What happens to Merlin Van Tornhout when he picks up a fellow Klansman on the way to a KKK meeting?

Assignment 4

Act 4

1. What is Leanora's relationship with Mr. Field?
2. What does Harvey do that makes Viola angry?
3. Who is Jerry? What happens to him?
4. What threat did Reynard Alexander receive?
5. What holiday does Esther enjoy celebrating?
6. Why does Johnny Reeves get kicked out of the KKK?
7. Why does the KKK think the Hirsh family is worse than the Sutter family?
8. What does the KKK want Merlin Van Tornhout to do?
9. What happens to Ira Hirsh?
10. Why does Merlin Van Tornhout run away?

Assignment 5

Act 5

1. How does Leanora know that Merlin didn't shoot Ira Hirsh?
2. Who saw the person who shot Ira Hirsh?
3. What does the KKK do to Johnny Reeves?
4. What does Percelle Johnson find in a box behind the tree?
5. Why doesn't Iris tell anyone that she saw Merlin while she was in New York?
6. What finally happens to Johnny Reeves?
7. What does Mr. Field do when he sees three Klansmen at the courthouse?
8. Why does Merlin return home?
9. Why does Merlin say he would never hurt Mr. Hirsh?
10. What surprise does Leanora get in the mail?
11. Who clears Merlin's name and provides evidence that he did not shoot Ira Hirsh?

STUDY GUIDE QUESTIONS ANSWER KEY *Witness*

Assignment 1

Act 1

1. Why are several young girls in the town upset about Miss Harvey's decision regarding "The Fountain of Youth"?
   Miss Harvey asks Leanora to dance in the production, but several of the girls don't want to dance with a black girl.
2. Who is Willie Pettibone?
   Willie is a white boy at school who hassles Leanora about her race.
3. How does Leanora's mother die?
   The night Leanora's family comes to town their wagon gets stuck in the mud. Leanora's dad goes to find help but no one wants to help a black man and his family. Leanora and her mother are left out in the cold for too long and Leanora's mother gets sick. She later dies from that illness.
4. Aside from liking Leanora despite her race, what sets Esther Hirsh apart from the other speakers in the novel?
   Esther's speech is very different from others'. She phrases her sentences in an odd structure.
5. Why does Leanora walk out into the cold without a coat, hat, or shoes?
   Willie tells Leanora the Klan is talking about burning both her and her father. She is so upset she walks out of school without her coat, hat, or shoes.
6. What does Sara Chickering do when Leanora shows up at her door in the freezing weather with no coat, hat, or shoes?
   Sara brings Leanora in, gives her warm broth and a blanket, and gives her a seat by the fire. Sara then runs a half mile into town to get the doctor and sends someone to get Leanora's father.
7. Iris Weaver owns her own restaurant but also has another, more secretive job. What is it?
   Iris smuggles alcohol into the town.
8. How do Harvey and Viola Pettibone feel about the Ku Klux Klan?
   Harvey wants to join the KKK, but his wife, Viola, is against the idea of being a member of such a violent group.
9. What happens to Lewis, a boy from school?
   While he is playing in a sandbank, it caves in. He is buried in it and suffocates.
10. What reason does Sara Chickering give for never marrying?
    She says she watched her mother work hard all the time while her father occasionally got breaks from his work. She saw her mother work harder to keep a household in order than her father ever did at his job.

Assignment 2

Act 2

1. Who is Bobby Franks?
   Bobby Franks is a rich, white boy from Chicago who is murdered. His murderers wanted ransom, but he is already dead when the ransom note is sent.
2. Why does Leanora help Mr. Field?
   Mr. Field has been feeling sick. Leanora's father sends her to help him.

3. Where does Esther think her mother is?
She thinks her mother took a train to heaven.
4. Harvey Pettibone tells his wife about what Johnny Reeves was preaching in his store earlier that day. What does Johnny say about women and happiness?
Harvey says Johnny Reeves was telling the men of the town to get their families out of the restaurant and back to the dinner table. Johnny says that women might have been distracted while out earning wages and working, but women are most happy when they are at home taking care of their families.
5. What has Iris Weaver done with the money she has made smuggling in illegal alcohol?
She has paid for the restaurant she owns and has made enough money to send her two brothers and one sister to college.
6. Mr. Field offers Leanora gifts that she would love to have. Each time he offers her something she wants, she declines his offer. Why doesn't she take his gifts when she wants them so much?
She knows that if she walks from Mr. Field's neighborhood to her neighborhood with something expensive, everyone would assume she stole it. She doesn't think having the gift is worth the trouble it would probably bring.
7. Why does Merlin Van Tornhout get arrested?
His 15-year-old girlfriend wrote him a letter from the orphanage begging him to rescue her and get married. He went and got her and was later arrested for kidnapping.
8. When does the KKK set the cross on fire?
It happens at the Independence Day concert, just after the band has played The Star-Spangled Banner for the families in town.
9. What groups does the KKK target?
The KKK targets Catholics, Jewish people, and black people with their hate.
10. Why does Ira Hirsh consider moving out of Sara Chickering's house?
Someone throws a rock through Sara's window with a note attached. He wants to move out of the house so that the KKK will leave Sara alone.

Assignment 3

<u>Act 3</u>

1. What happens when Iris Weaver gets caught with illegal alcohol in her car?
The man who is in the car with her takes the blame, saying the alcohol is all his.
2. What does the KKK do to keep up the appearance that they are serving the community?
They deliver baskets to the needy and give money to the poor.
3. Why does Esther stand on the railroad tracks and refuse to move as a train approaches?
She was told her mother took a train to heaven. She thinks that all people who die get to heaven by train, and she wants to stop the train so she can get on and take her mother some flowers in heaven.
4. Why is there an article about Leanora in the newspaper?
She saves Esther by pushing her out of the way of the train at the last second. She is considered a town hero and is featured in the newspaper for her good deed.
5. Leanora's father gets a threatening letter in the mail. What does it say?
The letter warns him to leave town. The person who wrote it threatens to tie both Leanora and Esther to the train tracks.
6. What does the KKK have against Esther and her father?
They are Jewish.

7. The lawyer who is arguing Leopold and Loeb's trial is not arguing that they were innocent. He admits they were guilty. What is his argument instead?
   Their lawyer is arguing against the death penalty. He doesn't think the state should ever take a human being's life.
8. What could Merlin Van Tornhout do to advance in the KKK?
   He could give them the keys to the newspaper since he works there and has access to everything.
9. What ends up happening to Leopold and Loeb, the two boys being tried for the murder of Bobby Franks?
   They are both found guilty but are not sentenced to death since the judge in charge of the case doesn't believe in the death penalty for minors.
10. Harvey puts brooms on sale for one penny and women stampede his store to get one. Twelve women are injured as a result and have to go to the doctor for medical attention. Viola says the doctor might just charge Harvey for the medical bills, since he hasn't been too happy with him lately. What does Harvey say will happen if the doctor unfairly tries to charge him for the medical bills?
    He says the KKK will take care of the doctor if he treats Harvey unfairly.
11. What happens to Merlin Van Tornhout when he picks up a fellow Klansman on the way to a KKK meeting?
    The man gets in the car and pulls out a knife, making Merlin get out so he can have his car.

Assignment 4

Act 4

1. What is Leanora's relationship with Mr. Field?
   She becomes friends with him and enjoys listening to him talk.
2. What does Harvey do that makes Viola angry?
   He goes into a hotel with other Klan members and smashes bottles, doing $400 worth of damage.
3. Who is Jerry? What happens to him?
   Jerry is Sara Chickering's dog that is killed one night.
4. What threat did Reynard Alexander receive?
   He received a letter that told him to be careful what he printed in the newspaper, or the day would come he would not print or say anything again.
5. What holiday does Esther enjoy celebrating?
   Esther enjoys celebrating Halloween.
6. Why does Johnny Reeves get kicked out of the KKK?
   His mother gives Harvey a letter saying she caught him in an inappropriate situation with a young school girl. The KKK won't tolerate that type of behavior, so he is kicked out.
7. Why does the KKK think the Hirsh family is worse than the Sutter family?
   Though the Sutters are black, the KKK is angrier at the Hirsh family for staining a pure Christian woman by living with her. They are angry the Jewish family is living with Sara.
8. What does the KKK want Merlin Van Tornhout to do?
   They want him to put rat poison in the Sutters' well.
9. What happens to Ira Hirsh?
   He is shot while he is sitting at the kitchen table with Esther on his lap.

10. Why does Merlin Van Tornhout run away?
    Harvey tells him that if he couldn't put the rat poison in the Sutters' well, then he better run because the Klan would come after him.

Assignment 5

<u>Act 5</u>

1. How does Leanora know that Merlin didn't shoot Ira Hirsh?
   Leanora saw Merlin outside her house near their well at the same time he supposedly shot Ira Hirsh.
2. Who saw the person who shot Ira Hirsh?
   Esther saw the man who shot her father.
3. What does the KKK do to Johnny Reeves?
   They brand his back with the letters "KKK."
4. What does Percelle Johnson find in a box behind the tree?
   He finds a baby girl that is two days old wrapped in newspaper and stuffed in a shoe box, left to die.
5. Why doesn't Iris tell anyone that she saw Merlin while she was in New York?
   If she tells them where she saw Merlin, she would have to explain what she was doing there, and then she would get caught for smuggling alcohol.
6. What finally happens to Johnny Reeves?
   He commits suicide by jumping off the highest point on the bridge.
7. What does Mr. Field do when he sees three Klansmen at the courthouse?
   He attacks them with his cane.
8. Why does Merlin return home?
   He is tired of running. He thinks he sees Johnny Reeves chasing him every place he goes.
9. Why does Merlin say he would never hurt Mr. Hirsh?
   Mr. Hirsh gave him a pair of galoshes to give to his girlfriend, and he could never hurt someone who made his girlfriend so happy.
10. What surprise does Leanora get in the mail?
    She gets a signed book from Helen Keller in response to the letter she wrote.
11. Who clears Merlin's name and provides evidence that he did not shoot Ira Hirsh?
    Leanora confesses that Merlin did not do the crime and provides evidence that he is innocent.

MULTIPLE CHOICE STUDY/QUIZ QUESTIONS

Witness

Assignment 1
Act 1

1. Why are several young girls in the town upset about Miss Harvey's decision regarding "The Fountain of Youth"?
   A. They want to perform a more modern play instead of something so old.
   B. The don't want black people to be able to sit next to the fountain or swim in it.
   C. They don't want to dance with a black girl.
   D. They want to put a statue of an elegant swan in the middle instead of an old man.

2. Who is Willie Pettibone?
   A. Willie is the only white person at school who is friends with Leanora.
   B. Wille is a white boy at school who has a crush on Leanora.
   C. Willie is a white boy at school who hassles Leanora about her race.
   D. Willie is the only other black person in the school and can relate to what Leanora is gong through.

3. How does Leanora's mother die?
   A. The KKK targets Leanora's family. Instead of allowing them to hurt Leanora, her mother confronts them and sacrifices herself to save her daughter.
   B. The family wagon gets stuck in the mud. Leanora's father goes to get help but can't find anyone who will help a black family. Her mother is out in the cold for too long and she gets sick; she later dies from the illness.
   C. She is walking to the grocery store when three white men begin harassing her. She tries to run away but they catch her and push her around. She falls and hits her head on a rock, and they leave her to bleed to death.
   D. She commits suicide because she could not handle the constant racial tension and threats.

4. Aside from liking Leanora despite her race, what sets Esther Hirsh apart from the other speakers in the novel?
   A. Her speech is very different from others'.
   B. She only says one or two words at a time.
   C. She has very long, drawn out speeches, lapsing several pages.
   D. She is the only person in the town who has lived in another city.

5. Why does Leanora walk out into the cold without a coat, hat, or shoes?
   A. Viola catches Leanora stealing from her shop. Leanora drops her winter coat and hat on the floor and runs out of the store, forgetting her boots by the door.
   B. Willie tells Leanora that the KKK is talking about burning her and her father. She is so upset she walks out of school without her outerwear.
   C. Leanora's father yells at her and forces her to go back to school. She is so angry at him she storms out of the house without protection from the cold.
   D. Leanora hears Esther screaming in the barn next to her house. She is so concerned about her friend she runs out without protection from the cold.

6. What does Sara Chickering do when Leanora shows up at her door in freezing weather with no coat, hat, or shoes?
   A. She takes Leanora back to her father wrapped in a blanket.
   B. She give Leanora a coat and sends her home.
   C. Sara gives her warm broth and sits her by the fire while she runs to town to get help and sends someone for Leanora's father.
   D. She gives her money to buy new clothes and supplies for school.

7. Iris Weaver owns her own restaurant but also has another, more secretive job. What is it?
   A. Running a large gambling ring
   B. Organizing KKK meetings
   C. Managing a popular jazz club
   D. Smuggling alcohol into town

8. How do Harvey and Viola Pettibone feel about the Ku Klux Klan?
   A. They both want to join.
   B. Viola wants to join and Harvey doesn't.
   C. Harvey wants to join and Viola doesn't.
   D. They are both against joining.

9. What happens to Lewis, a boy from school?
   A. He is shot while walking home.
   B. He is suffocated when a sandbank caves in around him.
   C. He dies after spending the night outside in the cold.
   D. He is kicked in the head by a horse.

10. What reason does Sara Chickering give for never marrying?

A. She doesn't want children and has never met a man who feels the same way.

B. She has never found anyone who she thought is worthy enough to marry.

C. She owns her own farm and has never found a man who isn't intimidated by her success.

D. She watched her mom work harder running the house than her father ever did working and doesn't want to end up the same way.

Assignment 2
Act 2

1. Who is Bobby Franks?
   A. A rich, white boy from Chicago who murdered a black girl
   B. A rich, white boy from Chicago who was murdered
   C. A poor, black boy from Chicago who murdered a white girl
   D. A poor, black boy from Chicago who was murdered

2. Why does Leanora help Mr. Field?
   A. He is the oldest man in town and needs help around the house. Leanora's teacher told the class about him, and she is helping him for community service.
   B. Leanora needs the $10 a week he has agreed to pay her. Money is tight at home, and she wants to help out as much as possible.
   C. Mr. Field has been sick. Leanora's father sends her to help him.
   D. Leanora is lonely and is hoping he will become her friend. She feels like she needs someone to talk to since so many people ignore her.

3. Where does Esther think her mother is?
   A. She thinks her mother is staying with a friend.
   B. She thinks her mother is working in another town.
   C. She has no idea where her mother is.
   D. She thinks she took a train to heaven.

4. Harvey Pettibone tells his wife about what Johnny Reeves was preaching in his store earlier that day. What does Johnny say about women and happiness?
   A. Women may have enjoyed taking care of their families, but they are really most happy working in the mills and factories.
   B. Women might have been distracted while working during the war, but they are really most happy back at home taking care of their families.
   C. Women might have been happy taking care of their families, but they are really most happy when they are part of the Klan.
   D. Women might have been happy just taking care of children, but they are really most happy when helping the church.

5. What has Iris Weaver done with the money she has made smuggling in illegal alcohol?
   A. She has paid for the restaurant she owns and has made enough money to buy a new car.
   B. She has bought expensive clothing and has gambled the rest away.
   C. She has paid for the restaurant she owns and has made enough money to send her two brothers and one sister to college.
   D. She has bought robes for all the Klan members and has helped fund the KKK in Vermont.

6. Mr. Field offers Leanora gifts that she would love to have. Each time he offers her something she wants, she declines his offer. Why doesn't she take his gifts when she wants them so much?

   A. She thinks it is improper for a black girl to take gifts from a white man.
   B. By taking the gifts she would feel obligated to continue working for him at a time when she is hoping to stop soon.
   C. She is worried people will think she is stealing the items from him.
   D. Her father won't let her take handouts from others. He thinks they are doing just fine on their own.

7. For what does Merlin Van Tornhout get arrested?

   A. He is arrested for breaking into the church.
   B. He is arrested for setting a cross on fire outside of Leanora's home.
   C. He is arrested for kidnapping his girlfriend.
   D. He is arrested for stealing from Harvey Pettibone's store.

8. When does the KKK set the cross on fire?

   A. It happens in the evening as the Jewish Synagogue is letting out.
   B. It happens at the end of the Independence Day concert.
   C. It happens in the middle of the night while everyone is asleep.
   D. It happens in the early morning while people are waking up and beginning their chores about town.

9. What groups does the KKK target?

   A. Protestants, black people, and foreigners
   B. Catholics, black people, and Jewish people
   C. Catholics, poor people, and black people
   D. Protestants, black people, and poor people

10. Why does Ira Hirsh consider moving out of Sara Chickering's house?

   A. Sara has been comparing him to other men she has known in the past. He is worried she is starting to have feelings for him and wants to leave to avoid hurting her.
   B. Esther is getting too attached to Sara. He is worried that his daughter will keep bothering her and wants to leave before they wear out their welcome.
   C. Business is slow at the shoe store since many people in the Klan are boycotting his store. He can no longer afford to pay Sara a fair amount and wants to leave to allow her to rent his room to someone who can pay her.
   D. Someone throws a rock through Sara's window with a note attached. He wants to move out of the house so that the KKK will leave Sara alone.

Assignment 3
Act 3

1. What happens when Iris Weaver gets caught with illegal alcohol in her car?
   A. The cop arrests her and takes her to jail.
   B. She pays the cop half her profit in exchange for looking the other way.
   C. She runs into the woods to avoid being arrested.
   D. The man who is in the car with her takes the blame, saying the alcohol is his.

2. What does the KKK do to keep up the appearance that they are serving the community?
   A. They buy clothes and school supplies for kids who come from poor families.
   B. They deliver baskets the needy and give money to the poor.
   C. They help the church raise money for the poor.
   D. All the members attend church regularly.

3. Why does Esther stand on the railroad tracks and refuse to move as a train approaches?
   A. She misses her friends and family in New York but doesn't have enough money to visit them. She stands on the tracks hoping the train conductor will feel bad for her and let her go to New York for free.
   B. She was told her mother took a train to heaven. She thinks that all people who die get to heaven by train, and she wants to stop the train so she can get on and take her mother some flowers in heaven.
   C. She finds a litter of baby kittens on the train tracks and is trying to save them. As the train approaches, she stands in the way to stop it before it hits the kittens.
   D. She enjoys the circus animals so much she wants to see them one last time before they leave town. The animals have been loaded on the train, and she tries to stop it.

4. Why is there an article about Leanora in the newspaper?
   A. In an article about The Fountain of Youth dance, Leanora is mentioned as the only black dancer.
   B. Mr. Field wrote an article about Leanora expressing how much he appreciates all her help.
   C. She saves Esther from being struck by a train.
   D. The Klan is trying to run her and her family out of town.

5. Leanora's father gets a threatening letter in the mail. What does it say?
   A. Leanora's father receives a letter warning him to leave town or something may happen to Leanora and Esther.
   B. Leanora's father receives a letter warning him to take Leanora out of school or something may happen to her.
   C. Leanora's father receives a letter warning him to close his shop or they will close it for him.
   D. Leanora's father receives a letter warning him to leave town or something may happen to him.

6. What does the KKK have against Esther and her father?
   A. They are known for helping black people.
   B. They are black.
   C. They are Jewish.
   D. They organize groups to fight the KKK.

7. The lawyer who is arguing Leopold and Loeb's trial is not arguing that they were innocent. He admits they were guilty. What is he arguing for instead?
   A. A jail sentence instead of the death penalty
   B. A shorter jail sentence
   C. A plea bargain if they name the leader of the KKK
   D. No jail time beacuse they are both insane

8. What could Merlin Van Tornhout do to advance in the KKK?
   A. Give them the keys to the newspaper office
   B. Help them steal more wood to make crosses
   C. Vandalize Ira Hirsh's shoe shop
   D. Kill Leanora's father

9. What ends up happening to Leopold and Loeb, the two boys being tried for the murder of Bobby Franks?
   A. The KKK breaks into the jail and kills both boys.
   B. They are found guilty but not sentenced to death since they are minors.
   C. They are found guilty and are sentenced to death by hanging.
   D. They are allowed to go free since the jury thinks they are clinically insane.

10. Harvey puts brooms on sale for one penny and women stampede his store to get one. Twelve women are injured as a result and have to go to the doctor for medical attention. Viola says the doctor might just charge Harvey for the medical bills, since the doctor hasn't been too happy with him lately. What does Harvey say will happen if the doctor unfairly tries to charge him for the medical bills?

   A. Harvey will take the doctor to court and sue him.
   B. The KKK will cover any expenses Harvey is responsible for.
   C. Harvey will refuse to pay and go to another doctor.
   D. The KKK will take care of the doctor if he treats Harvey unfairly.

11. What happens to Merlin Van Tornhout when he picks up a fellow Klansman on the way to a KKK meeting?

   A. The man tells Merlin he will help get him promoted to a higher positon in the KKK.
   B. The man pulls out a knife and steals Merlin's car.
   C. The man beats up Merlin and steals his wallet.
   D. The man agrees to help Merlin get his girlfriend out of the orphanage.

Assignment 4
Act 4

1. What is Leanora's relationship with Mr. Field?
   A. She gets bored with all his rambling and wishes he would hurry and get better.
   B. She begins to hate him since he obviously doesn't like black people.
   C. She starts to look at him as more of a father than her real dad.
   D. She becomes friends with him and enjoys listening to him talk.

2. What does Harvey do that makes Viola angry?
   A. He and other Klan members break all the windows in the Catholic church, doing $600 worth of damage.
   B. He goes into a hotel with other Klan members and smashes bottles, doing $400 worth of damage.
   C. He breaks into Ira Hirsh's shoe store with other Klan members and vandalizes his store, doing $200 worth of damage.
   D. He and other Klan members burn a cross on the Sutters' lawn. The land is dry and the fire spreads, doing $800 worth of damage.

3. Identify Jerry and tell what happens to him.
   A. A cow that belongs to Sara and is shot for eating another farmer's crops
   B. A black boy from Chicago who is hanged by the Klan
   C. Sara's dog that is killed one night
   D. A white boy from Memphis who is convicted of killing two black men

4. What threat did Reynard Alexander receive?
   A. To hand over the ownership of the newspaper or something bad will happen to him
   B. To be careful what he prints in the newspaper or something bad will happen to him
   C. To stop printing a daily newspaper or something bad will happen to him
   D. To print a KKK advertisement in the newspaper or something bad will happen to him

5. What holiday does Esther enjoy celebrating?
   A. Thanksgiving
   B. Halloween
   C. Easter
   D. Christmas

6. Why does Johnny Reeves get kicked out of the KKK?
   A. They are tired of him being too controlling and dominant. He is kicked out so someone else can take power.
   B. His mother writes a letter saying she caught him in an inappropriate situation with a young school girl. He gets kicked out because they won't tolerate that type of behavior.
   C. A "loose" woman shows up claiming that Johnny is the father of her baby. He gets kicked out for being an immoral man.
   D. He backs out of helping kill Mr. Sutter. His disobedience gets him kicked out.

7. Why does the KKK think the Hirsh family is worse than the Sutter family?
   A. Esther is always wandering around town causing more of a problem than Leanora who actually helps take care of the sick white people in town.
   B. They hate Jewish people more than black people.
   C. The Hirsh family lives with a white woman and the KKK blames them for staining a pure woman's name.
   D. Ira owns his own business and is taking money away from white people, while Mr. Sutter is a laborer the town needs to do hard work.

8. What does the KKK want Merlin Van Tornhout to do?
   A. Kidnap Esther
   B. Beat up Leanora
   C. Put poison in the Sutters' well
   D. Burn down Mr. Hirsh's shoe store

9. What happens to Ira Hirsh?
   A. He is shot.
   B. He is tarred and feathered.
   C. He is hanged.
   D. He is severely beaten.

10. Why does Merlin Van Tornhout run away?
   A. He can't follow through with what the Klan wants him to do, so Harvey tells him to leave town before the Klan comes after him.
   B. His father is beating him, and he can't take it anymore.
   C. He is tired of being a part of the Klan and wants out. He knows he wouldn't be able to just quit, so he runs away.
   D. He runs away to be with his girlfriend, Mary. The two work out a plan to get married without anyone knowing.

Assignment 5
Act 5

1. How does Leanora know that Merlin didn't shoot Ira Hirsh?
   A. She saw Merlin outside her house at the same time he supposedly shot Mr. Hirsh.
   B. She saw the person who really did do it as he left the Hirsh's house that night.
   C. She knows Merlin doesn't know how to shoot a gun and wouldn't have the aim.
   D. She is good friends with him, and he told her he didn't do it.

2. Who saw the person who shot Ira Hirsh?
   A. Iris Weaver
   B. Harvey Pettibone
   C. Esther Hirsh
   D. Leanora Sutter

3. What does the KKK do to Johnny Reeves?
   A. They brand his back with the letters "KKK."
   B. They tar and feather him.
   C. They kill his mother.
   D. They vandalize his church.

4. What does Percelle Johnson find in a box behind the tree?
   A. The stolen goods from the church
   B. Four Klansman suits ripped to shreds
   C. A baby that was left to die
   D. The kittens Sara Chickering has tried to get rid of

5. Why doesn't Iris tell anyone that she saw Merlin while she was in New York?
   A. She wasn't exactly sure it was him and didn't want to get anyone's hopes up.
   B. She worries if she tells someone where he is, they will go after him and arrest him for shooting Ira Hirsh.
   C. She knows if she tells someone were she saw him, she would have to explain why she was there and might get caught for smuggling alcohol.
   D. She respects his privacy and knows he will come back when he has sorted his problems out.

6. What finally happens to Johnny Reeves?
   A. He is found hanging from a tree.
   B. He is arrested for his inappropriate actions with the young school girl.
   C. He runs off to search for Merlin.
   D. He commits suicide by jumping off the highest point of the bridge.

7. What does Mr. Field do when he sees three Klansmen at the courthouse?
   A. He attacks them with his cane.
   B. He salutes them to show respect.
   C. He tries to get away as quickly as possible without causing any trouble.
   D. He asks if he can join the Klan.

8. Why does Merlin return home?
   A. He is tired of running. He thinks he sees Johnny Reeves chasing him every place he goes.
   B. An old preacher convinces Merlin to stop running and go back home. He tells Merlin to tell the truth and everything will work out in the end.
   C. He discovers his mother is very ill and comes back to be with her.
   D. A warrant for arrest is out in his name. If he turns himself in, he has as better chance at explaining himself and getting a lighter sentence.

9. Why does Merlin say he would never hurt Mr. Hirsh?
   A. His father was also in the shoe business before he died. To honor his father, he could never hurt someone in the same profession.
   B. Mr. Hirsh saved Merlin when he fell through the ice one winter. Merlin is alive because of Mr. Hirsh and could never hurt him.
   C. His ancestors on his mother's side were Jewish, and he could never hurt a Jewish person for that reason.
   D. Mr. Hirsh gave him a pair of galoshes to give to his girlfriend, and he could never hurt someone who made his girlfriend so happy.

10. What surprise does Leanora get in the mail?
   A. She receives new dancing shoes from an anonymous person.
   B. She receives a letter of apology from Merlin.
   C. She receives a signed book from Helen Keller.
   D. She receives the typewriter Mr. Fields had that she wanted so badly.

11. Who clears Merlin's name and provides evidence that he did not shoot Ira Hirsh?
   A. Esther Hirsh
   B. Sara Chickering
   C. Mr. Sutter
   D. Leanora Sutter

ANSWER KEY: STUDY QUESTIONS *Witness*

	1	2	3	4	5
1	C	B	D	D	A
2	C	C	B	B	C
3	B	D	B	C	A
4	A	B	C	B	C
5	B	C	A	B	C
6	C	C	C	B	D
7	D	C	A	C	A
8	C	B	A	C	A
9	B	B	B	A	D
10	D	D	D	A	C
11			B		D

VOCABULARY WORKSHEETS

VOCABULARY ASSIGNMENT 1 *Witness*

Part I: Using Prior Knowledge and Contextual Clues

Below are the sentences in which the vocabulary words appear in the text. Read the sentence. Use any clues you can find in the sentence combined with your prior knowledge, and write what you think the underlined words mean on the lines provided.

1. Percelle Johnson, town constable (aged 66)

2. Johnny Reeves, clergyman (aged 36)

3. doc flitt said she ought to go away to a sanatorium to get her health back.

4. they even tried him, neighbor, they tried him before a jury of white men for inciting trouble, for leading the lord's sheep to stray, and still, neighbor, it grieves me to tell you that still, they let the devil go free.

5. they even tried him, neighbor, they tried him before a jury of white men for inciting trouble, for leading the lord's sheep to stray, and still, neighbor, it grieves me to tell you that still, they let the devil go free.

6. my daddy says *revealed jesus* better get his brave behind up north pretty quick because what he's doing down there in texas is sure to get him lynched.

7. though she drinks cocktails and shows an inordinate fondness for lipstick and rouge pot, we have nothing to fear.

8. this paper is neutral. this editor is neutral. i have attempted to remain neutral in the face of the klan question and i intend to continue neutral until i have reason to do otherwise.

9. we shall reign in the kingdom, neighbor. we shall form a great fist, and we shall still those who oppose us.

10. every lamb, once he has known the light, cannot endure the darkness.

Witness Vocabulary Worksheet Assignment 1 Continued

Part II: Determining the Meaning -- Match the vocabulary words to their dictionary definitions.

____ 1.	CONSTABLE	A. Christian minister
____ 2.	CLERGYMAN	B. Institution for the treatment of certain chronic diseases or various nervous or mental disorders
____ 3.	SANATORIUM	C. Belonging to neither side in a controversy
____ 4.	INCITING	D. Peace officer with less authority than a sheriff
____ 5.	GRIEVES	E. Hanged, as by a mob, without due process of the law
____ 6.	LYNCHED	F. Feels sorrow or distress
____ 7.	INORDINATE	G. Stirring up, encouraging or prompting into action
____ 8.	NEUTRAL	H. Exceeding reasonable limits; uncontrolled
____ 9.	REIGN	I. Rule or hold authority; dominate with power or influence
____ 10.	ENDURE	J. Carry on despite hardships

VOCABULARY ASSIGNMENT 2 *Witness*

Part I: Using Prior Knowledge and Contextual Clues

Below are the sentences in which the vocabulary words appear in the text. Read the sentence. Use any clues you can find in the sentence combined with your prior knowledge, and write what you think the underlined words mean on the lines provided.

1. if leopold had not dropped his spectacles, if the spectacles had not been so uncommon, they would have gotten away with it.

   ____

2. mr. field said: i saw the brigade of negroes under general burnside. like a long streamer of dark silk they were.

   ____

3. the fire took off so fast. a divine sight, neighbor, the flames spread from the base to the top.

   ____

4. the flames leaping, seeking heaven, neighbor, the white crucifix scoring the night blazed perfect. perfect.

   ____

5. the kerosene took off so fast. burned so fierce. christ. i can still see it when i close my eyes.

   ____

6. only a lunatic would ignore the dry conditions, or the fact that a crackling fire could spread so easily out of control.

   ____

7. or perhaps it was the work of children stirred by griffith's *birth of a nation,* that racist rubbish, which will not fade away.

   ____

8. sara chickering did grumble about men in their nightshirts with their filthy wet hems and i did laugh at her so serious....

   ____

9. klan can seem mighty right-minded, with their talk of family virtue, mighty decent, if you don't scratch the surface. there's a kind of power they wield, a deceptive authority.

   ____

10. klan can seem mighty right-minded, with their talk of family virtue, mighty decent, if you don't scratch the surface. there's a kind of power they wield, a deceptive authority.

   ____

Witness Vocabulary Worksheet Assignment 2 Continued

Part II: Determining the Meaning -- Match the vocabulary words to their dictionary definitions.

____ 1.	SPECTACLES	A.	Exercise power, or influence as in ruling or dominating
____ 2.	BRIGADE	B.	Large body of troops; a military unit
____ 3.	DIVINE	C.	Insane person
____ 4.	CRUCIFIX	D.	A cross with the form of Jesus on it
____ 5.	FIERCE	E.	Eyeglasses
____ 6.	LUNATIC	F.	Misleading; to make others believe something that is not true
____ 7.	RUBBISH	G.	Furiously intense; wild; violent in force
____ 8.	GRUMBLE	H.	Supremely good or beautiful; magnificent
____ 9.	WIELD	I.	Muttering a complaint
____ 10.	DECEPTIVE	J.	Nonsense; worthless material; garbage

VOCABULARY ASSIGNMENT 3 *Witness*

Part I: Using Prior Knowledge and Contextual Clues

Below are the sentences in which the vocabulary words appear in the text. Read the sentence. Use any clues you can find in the sentence combined with your prior knowledge, and write what you think the underlined words mean on the lines provided.

1. the klan appears to serve the best interest of the greater community, "cleaning" it up, keeping a vigilant eye out for loose morals and lawbreakers.

   ____

2. they deliver baskets to the needy, and money to the destitute.

   ____

3. from state to state, from town to town, men join who cannot be trusted. unscrupulous men who work in the dark behind hoods and masks.

   ____

4. i have reached the pinnacle, neighbor. tapped by the exalted dragons. i, neighbor, led the klan in their opening prayers.

   ____

5. i do have the prickle scratches on my legs and on my arm from where leanora did push me down in the tangle grass and sara chickering says in a big scold voice that i am never, never, ever stopping a train not ever, never, never on the train tracks.

   ____

6. pretty near everyone with a place backing the river came out, vexed from listening to it yowl.

   ____

7. caverly says his decision holds with the dictates of enlightened humanity.

   ____

8. how was i supposed to know they'd be so pushy over a broom sale? stinking stampede it was, vi.

   ____

9. the two stand facing off, each as stout and solid as a house.

   ____

Witness Vocabulary Worksheet Assignment 3 Continued

Part II: Determining the Meaning -- Match the vocabulary words to their dictionary definitions.

____ 1.	VIGILANT	A. Lacking food, clothing, and shelter
____ 2.	DESTITUTE	B. Guiding principles
____ 3.	UNSCRUPULOUS	C. Without principles
____ 4.	PINNACLE	D. On the alert; watchful
____ 5.	SCOLD	E. Firm; strong; having endurance
____ 6.	VEXED	F. The highest point, as with success, power, or fame
____ 7.	DICTATES	G. Frenzied rush of a mass of people
____ 8.	STAMPEDE	H. Reprimand or criticize harshly and usually angrily
____ 9.	STOUT	I. Irritated; annoyed

VOCABULARY ASSIGNMENT 4 *Witness*

Part I: Using Prior Knowledge and Contextual Clues

Below are the sentences in which the vocabulary words appear in the text. Read the sentence. Use any clues you can find in the sentence combined with your prior knowledge, and write what you think the underlined words mean on the lines provided.

1. he's thin as a broomstick, gangling tall, his eyes cloudy.

   ____

2. so you go in, dressed in those ku klux nightclothes of yours and you think you'll save the world from the evils of drink by raiding the place and smashing a few bottles?

   ____

3. a threat came from the klan, in the form of a letter, advising me to be careful what i print and what I say, or the day would come when i would not print or say anything again.

   ____

4. but surely the moment will pass, and the same ordinary, hardheaded, folks who invited them in, will sensibly suggest the klan pack up their poison and go.

   ____

5. one of the things i like best about mr. hirsh is that he didn't move himself up here thinking how rich he would get on the backs of some rustic vermonters.

   ____

6. sara chickering sounded rattled enough when she phoned from iris weaver's. sara chickering, who never gets rattled.

   ____

7. persecution is not american. it is not american to give the power of life and death to a secret organization.

   ____

8. ...i'm laughing, too. until the laughter turns on us and we are wringing grief, our faces touching, our hands entwined.

   ____

9. ...i'm laughing, too. until the laughter turns on us and we are wringing grief, our faces touching, our hands entwined.

   ____

10. says he came up on foot around dusk, peered through the keyhole in the kitchen door, saw mr. hirsh seated at the table with esther on his lap.

   ____

Witness Vocabulary Worksheet Assignment 4 Continued

Part II: Determining the Meaning -- Match the vocabulary words to their dictionary definitions.

____ 1.	GANGLING	A.	Recommending; suggesting
____ 2.	RAIDING	B.	Awkwardly tall or long-limbed
____ 3.	ADVISING	C.	Looked intently, searchingly, or with difficulty
____ 4.	SENSIBLY	D.	Typical of country life of country people
____ 5.	RUSTIC	E.	Punishment or harassment usually of a severe nature on the basis of race, religion, or political opinion
____ 6.	RATTLED	F.	Showing good sense or sound judgment
____ 7.	PERSECUTION	G.	Extracting or expelling by twisting or compression
____ 8.	WRINGING	H.	Flustered; unnerved; confused
____ 9.	ENTWINED	I.	Around or twisted together
____ 10.	PEERED	J.	Conducting a surprise attack on another's property with the purpose of taking goods

VOCABULARY ASSIGNMENT 5 *Witness*

Part I: Using Prior Knowledge and Contextual Clues

Below are the sentences in which the vocabulary words appear in the text. Read the sentence. Use any clues you can find in the sentence combined with your prior knowledge, and write what you think the underlined words mean on the lines provided.

1. he was branded on the back with the letters k.k.k. and was suffering from shock, unable to give any explanation of his condition.

 ____

2. now, though the klan does its best to stir up racial strife, there have been only five lynchings reported.

 ____

3. senator greene sent a letter to the press urging every man and woman to get out and vote for coolidge and dawes.

 ____

4. never before has a presidential candidate conducted himself during the campaign as did mr. coolidge.

 ____

5. i wouldn't hurt mr. hirsh. he gave me galoshes to bring to my girl, mary, when he heard about her walking halfway across the state, trying to get back home.

 ____

6. mary was so pleased she strutted around the orphanage like she was some kind of queen.

 ____

7. guess after everything else, when the government threw out the klan's petition they figured vermont wasn't such a good place for them after all.

 ____

8. they say winters demand less of us, and summers now are meek.

 ____

9. those who move away remember the massive town hall and solid stone church, the imposing brick schoolhouse.

 ____

10. to those who swear our young are on the road to perdition take comfort in this--every generation has felt somewhat the same for two or three thousand years and still the world goes on.

 ____

Witness Vocabulary Worksheet Assignment 5 Continued

Part II: Determining the Meaning -- Match the vocabulary words to their dictionary definitions.

____ 1.	BRANDED	A.	Waterproof boot or shoe
____ 2.	STRIFE	B.	Tame; gentle; kind
____ 3.	URGING	C.	Conflict; struggle; clash
____ 4.	CONDUCTED	D.	Formal request
____ 5.	GALOSHES	E.	Symbol burned on with a hot iron
____ 6.	STRUTTED	F.	Very impressive because of great size, stately appearance, or dignity
____ 7.	PETITION	G.	Future state of the wicked; damnation; hell
____ 8.	MEEK	H.	The way a person acts, especially from the standpoint of morality and ethics
____ 9.	IMPOSING	I.	Encouraging
____ 10.	PERDITION	J.	Walked in a pompous way

VOCABULARY ANSWER KEY - *Witness*

	1	2	3	4	5
1	D	E	D	B	E
2	A	B	A	J	C
3	B	H	C	A	I
4	G	D	F	F	H
5	F	G	H	D	A
6	E	C	I	H	J
7	H	J	B	E	D
8	C	I	G	G	B
9	I	A	E	I	F
10	J	F		C	G

DAILY LESSONS

LESSON ONE

Objectives

1. To introduce the *Witness* unit
2. To distribute books, study questions, and other related materials
3. To assign the unit project
4. To preview the vocabulary and study questions for Assignment 1

Activity 1

To prepare for this lesson, purchase several oranges of a similar size. Do not remove any stickers, and try to find oranges with distinguishing marks or coloring. Place the oranges in a bowl and have them for the start of class.

At the start of class select students to come up to the front of the room and select an orange from the bowl. Ask students to really study the orange they selected, making sure to note any marks or colors that could set it apart from the others. After giving students a few minutes to study their oranges, have students place the oranges back into the bowl. Ask your students to look away from the bowl and mix them up with your hand. Next, have the students turn back to the bowl and find the orange they just studied. Most students will be able to tell from stickers, discolorations, etc which orange was theirs. Have students briefly explain to the rest of the class how they identified their orange. Collect the oranges and place them back into the bowl and set it aside for the moment.

Distribute copies of *Witness* to students and ask them to take a few moments to look over the structure of the novel. Instruct them to read the first few pages where the characters are introduced with a photo and to try to determine how the novel is arranged structurally.

As students are becoming familiar with the novel, peel each of the oranges and place them back into the bowl. When you are finished, talk to your students regarding the structure of the story. Prompt them to discuss how the story is arranged, making sure to point out that it is a cross between a play, with varying speakers, and a series of poems with the odd arrangement of words and sentences.

Transition: When you have completed your discussion on the structure of the story, ask the same students to come to the front of the room to once again find their orange. Students will be unable to select their original orange since it will be peeled and all distinguishing marks gone. Explain to students that originally they were able to tell which orange was theirs based on its outside appearance, but once the orange was peeled, it was essentially the same as the others. Explain that each orange, though different on the outside, is as sweet and delicious as the next. Bridge the connection between the oranges to people. Talk to your students about judging others based on outward appearances and try to reinforce the idea that it is the personality, or the inside, that really matters. Once you have made this connection, tell students that they will be reading a story about people who are judged and are judging others based on their outward appearance. Talk to your students briefly about the racial and religious hatred they will encounter throughout the story.

Activity 2

Distribute the project requirements and discuss in detail.

Activity 3

Distribute the materials students will use in this unit. Explain in detail how students are to use these materials.

Study Guides Students should read the study guide questions for each reading assignment prior to beginning the reading assignment to get a feeling for what events and ideas are important in the section they are about to read. After reading the section, students will (as a class or individually) answer the questions to review the important events and ideas from that section of the book. Students should keep the study guides as study materials for the unit test. **Review the study questions for Assignment 1 while you're looking at the study guides.**

Vocabulary Prior to each reading assignment, students will do vocabulary work related to the section of the book they are about to read. Following the completion of the reading of the book, there will be a vocabulary review of all the words used in the vocabulary assignments. Students should keep their vocabulary work as study materials for the unit test. **Do Assignment 1 together orally to show students how to do the vocabulary worksheets.**

Reading Assignment Sheet You need to fill in the reading assignment sheet to let students know by when their reading has to be completed. You can either write the assignment sheet up on a side blackboard or bulletin board and leave it there for students to see each day, or you can make copies for each student to have. In either case, you should advise students to become very familiar with the reading assignments so they know what is expected of them.

Extra Activities Center The Unit Resource Materials portion of this LitPlan contains suggestions for an extra library of related books and articles in your classroom as well as crossword and word search puzzles. Make an extra activities center in your room where you will keep these materials for students to use. (Bring the books and articles in from the library and keep several copies of the puzzles on hand.) Explain to students that these materials are available for students to use when they finish reading assignments or other class work early.

Non-fiction Assignment Sheet Explain to students that they each are to read at least one non-fiction piece from the in-class library at some time during the unit. Students will fill out a Non-fiction Assignment Sheet after completing the reading to help you (the teacher) evaluate their reading experiences and to help the students think about and evaluate their own reading experiences.

Books Each school has its own rules and regulations regarding student use of school books. Advise students of the procedures that are normal for your school. Preview the book. Look at the covers, frontmatter, and index.

Activity 4
Since the story is written in play form, all the reading will take place in class to add emphasis to the many voices and perspectives in the story. It is recommended that you assign roles to students in advance so they may read over their part and develop a "voice" for their character.

During class readings, it may help to have all your students sitting in a circle. Since the roles in the play are written like poems and there is no narration or movement, students do not need to move or stand, but simply read their part. You may also want to make name cards for each character, so students avoid confusion as to which role each student is playing.

Another alternative would be to have all your students read the full act before each class so they understand the action in the play. You could then assign roles to willing students and read the act out loud to add to the effect of hearing different perspectives from the people in this town.

Decide how you will handle the assignment of roles and reading and give your class those instructions at this time. Allow them to begin reading with any remaining time.

UNIT PROJECT - *Witness*

Hate crimes are not a thing of the past, nor are they limited to crimes between races. Hate crimes have taken place throughout the course of history and continue to be a problem in the world today. Hate crimes occur between races, religions, genders, and various other groups. While reading Witness and learning about hate crimes and their victims in one part of the country, you will be studying hate crimes on your own. This project will prompt you to research hate crimes towards a specific group and then work to raise awareness about ending hate in your school community.

Step 1: Select one of the following topics for your project:

- Racial Hate Crimes
- Gender Based Hate Crimes
- Hate Crimes against people with disabilities or certain diseases
- Religious Hate Crimes
- Socioeconomic Hate Crimes
- Hate Crimes against people based on sexual orientation

Step 2: After selecting your topic, you will need to begin your research. The following items are what you will need to include in your project:

- Definition of Hate Crimes
- Current and past laws/legislation regarding hate crimes (both to your selected group and hate crimes in general)
- The different types of ha te crimes (acts of violence) that are commonly done against your selected group
- The history of hate crimes against your selected group in both the United States and the World
- Recent examples of hate crimes against your selected group in both the United States and the World
- Stories from victims (or their friends/families) who have experienced the type of hate crime you are researching
- Organizations who are working to combat this type of hate crime and information on what they are doing, where to get more information, and how others can help

Step 3: After finishing your research, find a creative way to present the information to the class. You may want to make a Power Point presentation, a brochure, a website, an information packet, or any other creative method you can think of to present your required information. Make sure to include all of the required information listed in step two along with pictures and other material to make your project stand out. Be prepared to present this information to the class.

Step 4: Create a poster to convince students to stop hate in your school community. Think of a catchy slogan or phrase to grab the attention of people passing by and use graphics as well. You may want to include statistics or information from your project or powerful quotes you find from victims, to appeal to others in your school. Your poster will then be hung in the classroom, and possibly around the school.

PART ASSIGNMENTS FOR *Witness*

PART	ACT ONE	ACT TWO	ACT THREE	ACT FOUR	ACT FIVE
LEANORA					
MERLIN					
ESTHER					
PERCELLE					
SARA					
JOHNNY					
IRIS					
FITZGERALD					
HARVEY					
VIOLA					
REYNARD					

LESSON TWO

Objectives

1. To teach students about the time period in which the story takes place
2. To provide background knowledge for terms and references found later in the novel

Activity

Witness takes place in the 1920's, a time period many students may not know about. The book references several social movements of the time, and students will need background knowledge to understand parts of the story.

One way to teach about this time period would be to check out a video from your school library detailing the time period. The History Channel has an interesting DVD available from their decade collection encompassing a variety of topics during the 1920's.

If you are able to view web sites with your students through a projector, or if you have a computer lab you can take your class to, you may want to teach about the time period via the web. The Library Think Quest site has a very detailed section of pages you can explore with your students. It is available at http://library.thinkquest.org/C005846/The_1920/the1920.htm.

These are just two suggestions for ways to teach your students about this time period. A simple Google search will bring up a wealth of information for you to use in your classroom, and several production companies have made educational videos on this period. Regardless of the method you choose, be sure to include information about the following topics before starting the book: The lifestyle (fashion, music, culture, flappers, speakeasy clubs, etc), racial tension and the KKK, the women's movement and the right to vote, and prohibition.

LESSON THREE

Objectives

1. To read Act 1
2. To practice oral reading
3. To spot-check students' reading comprehension

Activity

Place students in a circle and read Act 1 out loud. Remember to place name cards on the desks of those who have a role so other students are certain as to who each character is being played by. You may want to stop periodically throughout the reading to ask comprehension questions and be sure students are following along.

LESSON FOUR

Objectives

1. To review main ideas, events, and vocabulary of Assignment 1
2. To create a visual display that will be used as a during and after reading strategy
3. To help students organize the events of the story and the feelings and experiences of each character

Activity 1

Give students a few minutes to formulate answers for the study guide questions for Assignment 1, and then discuss the answers to the questions in detail. Write the answers on the board or overhead transparency so students can have the correct answers for study purposes.

NOTE: It is a good practice in public speaking and leadership skills for individual students to take charge of leading the discussions of the study questions. Perhaps a different student could go to the front of the class and lead the discussion each day that the study questions are discussed in this unit. Of course, you should guide the discussion when appropriate and try to fill in any gaps students may leave. The study questions could really be handled in a number of different ways, including in small groups with group reports following. Occasionally you may want to use the multiple choice questions as quizzes to check students' reading comprehension. As a short review now and then, students could pair up for the first (or last, if you have time left at the end of a class period) few minutes of class to quiz each other from the study questions. Mix up methods of reviewing the materials and checking comprehension throughout the unit so students don't get bored just answering the questions the same way each day. Variety in methods will also help address the different learning styles of your students. From now on in this unit, the directions will simply say, "Discuss the answers to the study questions in detail as previously directed." You will choose the method of preparation and discussion each day based on what best suits you and your class.

Activity 2

Review the vocabulary answers from the reading. Make sure students write down the correct answers.

Activity 3

Witness is told from the perspective of 11 different speakers. With so many different speakers and the story of each person jumping from page to page, the events in the story can get confusing for students. Students are also easily confused with the thoughts and feelings of each character, and where they stand in the issue of racial hatred in the community.

To help students with organizing the actions and feelings of each character, have students work in groups to create a cutout of each character. Place students in groups of two or three and assign each group a character from the story. Give them a large piece of bulletin board paper and have them make a cut out of that character. Instruct students to look at the photos in the front of the book to see the gender and age of each person to help with their cut out. Students may want to trace someone to make their cut out life-size, or sketch it by hand. Have students use markers to draw clothes and facial features for their character cut out. Once each character cut out is complete hang them on the walls of your classroom. Place a piece of large construction paper over each character's head with his or her name at the top. Leave plenty of blank space on the paper so students can add personality traits, thoughts, feelings, emotions, and actions of the characters as they read the novel.

Activity 4

Take a few moments to add information to your character cut outs from Act 1. Include information like character actions, memories, thoughts, feelings, interactions with other characters, opinions, etc. The point is to provide enough information from each act on the construction paper over the character so that students can stay organized with what is going on with each speaker in the text.

LESSON FIVE

Objectives

1. To have students research and read non-fiction related to the book to help connect the book to real life
2. To broaden students' knowledge about topics related to the book
3. To preview study questions and vocabulary for Assignment 2

Activity 1

Take students to the library or media center. With students, brainstorm a list of non-fiction topics that could be related to *Witness*. A short list to get you started is included below.

The KKK
Any aspect of the 1920's time period
Prohibition
Women's Rights Movement
Civil Rights Movement
Hate crimes in the past
Legislature on hate crimes
Victims of hate crimes
Hate crimes in the present (both in and out of the US)
Tolerance

Activity 2

Distribute the Non-fiction Assignment Sheet to students. Explain that students should choose a non-fiction topic related to *Witness.* They should read a substantial article related to that topic and complete the Non-fiction Assignment Sheet for that article. Students may use magazines, newspapers, and the Internet as sources.

Activity 3

Bring the class back together and have each student tell what he/she read about.

Note: Compiling the Non-fiction Assignment Sheets into a booklet makes a nice follow-up activity and a handy reference for students.

Activity 4

Review the study questions and vocabulary for Assignment 2 orally together in class. Tell students they should read Assignment 2 prior to the next class period.

NON-FICTION ASSIGNMENT SHEET

(To be completed after reading the required non-fiction article)

Name ______________________________ Date ___________________________

Title of Non-fiction Read ____

Written By _____________________ Publication Date _______________________

I. Factual Summary: Write a short summary of the piece you read.

II. Vocabulary

1. With which vocabulary words in the piece did you encounter some degree of difficulty?

2. How did you resolve your lack of understanding with these words?

III. Interpretation: What was the main point the author wanted you to get from reading his work?

IV. Criticism

1. With which points of the piece did you agree or find easy to accept? Why?

2. With which points of the piece did you disagree or find difficult to believe? Why?

V. Personal Response: What do you think about this piece? <u>OR</u> How does this piece influence your ideas?

LESSON SIX

Objectives

1. To read Act 2
2. To practice oral reading

Activity

Place students in a circle and read Act 2 as previously directed.

LESSON SEVEN

Objectives

1. To review main ideas, events, and vocabulary of Assignment 2
2. To help students organize the events of the story and the feelings and experiences of each character
3. To practice writing to inform
4. To improve students' writing ability

Activity 1
Discuss the answers to the study questions for Assignment 2 in detail as previously directed.

Activity 2
Review the vocabulary answers from the reading. Make sure students write down the correct answers.

Activity 3
Add events from the reading to character cut outs as previously directed.

Activity 4
Distribute the RAFT writing assignment to students. Explain that the purpose of this assignment is to write to inform. Tell students they should select one of the scenarios listed for their first writing assignment. Explain that the "R" stands for the role they will take, or the point if view from which they are writing; the "A" stands for the audience to whom they are writing; the "F" stands for the format of their writing; and the "T" stands for the topic or task. Quickly go over the different scenarios available to them and give the remaining class time for students to complete the assignment.

Witness Writing Assignment – RAFT

Directions: Select one of the following writing situations to use as the topic for your essay.

Role The voice you take on as a writer; this is the perspective you are writing from	Audience Who you are writing to; this is the person that will be reading what you write	Format The form your writing will take; this is the type of writing you will complete	Topic/Task Your purpose for writing; this is the content or reason for your writing assignment
A Flapper	Self	Diary Entry	Lifestyle (both good and bad) of a flapper
A Bootlegger	Another Bootlegger	Secret Letter	Challenges of bootlegging and thoughts on how to get around prohibition
A Woman	Other Women	Advice Column	The changing expectations of women and the challenges of breaking away from the traditional mold
An African American	Society	Poem	Your personal feelings about living with the threat of the KKK
A Jewish Person	A Community Member	Dialogue	How it feels to be targeted by the KKK and how to handle the pressure
A Civil Rights Leader	A large gathering of people	Speech	Your vision for an equal society without hate crimes
A Women's Rights Leader	Men & Women in Society	Radio Commercial	Urging women to take advantage of their rights and pushing men to be supportive
A Jazz Musician	An audience in a club	Song Lyrics	About the lifestyles of people in this time
An Officer or Government Official	The people in his community	Newspaper Article	Reasons why people need to obey the prohibition laws and how you are dealing with the KKK
The Owner of a Speakeasy	Young people in the city	Secret Advertisement	Reasons to forget about prohibition and come enjoy a night at the club; description of activities and people at the club

WRITING ASSIGNMENT #1 *Witness*

PROMPT
Select one of the scenarios listed on the RAFT writing assignment for the topic of your essay. The role is the point of view from which you are writing, the audience is to whom you are writing, the format is the type of writing you are doing, and the topic/task is the actual information you are writing about.

PREWRITING
After you have selected your writing scenario, begin to brainstorm ideas. Remember to think about the role from which you are writing, and the topic you are writing about. Use your book, notes about the time period, and notes from the non-fiction articles to help you with your support.

DRAFTING
Write an introductory paragraph that allows the reader to know the role you have assumed and the audience to whom you are writing. Give a general overview of the points you will make in the body paragraphs of your writing. Use the format of your writing to guide you on how to begin (speech would begin with a little about yourself, letter begins with Dear _______, etc).

In the body paragraphs, give the details of your topic. Use information from the novel, the speaker, and the non-fiction article you read to help provide support. Be sure to reread the topic/task you are writing about and be sure to cover all portions listed there.

In your conclusion paragraph, summarize your main points and conclude the writing assignment. For unity with your writing, you may want to tie in your role and audience once again.

PROMPT
When you finish the rough draft of your composition, ask a student who sits near you to read it. After reading your rough draft, he/she should tell you what he/she liked best about your work, which parts were difficult to understand, and ways in which your work could be improved. Reread your paper considering your critic's comments, and make the corrections you think are necessary. Ask your classmate what he/she thought of each of the characters/events you chose for your assignment.

PROOFREADING
Do a final proofreading of your paper double-checking your grammar, spelling, organization, and the clarity of your ideas.

WRITING EVALUATION FORM - *Witness*

Name ______________________________ Date ________________________

Writing Assignment # _______ Grade _________________

Circle One For Each Item:

Introduction:	excellent	good	fair	poor
Body Paragraphs:	excellent	good	fair	poor
Conclusion:	excellent	good	fair	poor
Grammar:	excellent	good	fair	poor
Spelling:	excellent	good	fair	poor
Punctuation:	excellent	good	fair	poor
Legibility:	excellent	good	fair	poor
Persuasiveness:	excellent	good	fair	poor
_____________	excellent	good	fair	poor

Strengths:

Weaknesses:

Comments/Suggestions:

LESSON EIGHT

<u>Objectives</u>

1. To bring ideas from the book into real life
2. To preview study questions and vocabulary for Assignment 3

<u>Activity 1</u>
This day is for a guest speaker. Invite one or more of the following people from your community to speak to your class:

Someone who has been the victim of a hate crime
An expert on hate crimes
An advocacy group working to end hate and teach tolerance
A police officer who has dealt with hate crime investigations
A political official from your state or county involved with legislature regarding hate crimes

Divide your class time according to how many speakers you're able to acquire. Remember to allow time for students to ask questions. Let each speaker know how much time he/she will have for the presentation. Allow for time at the end of the class for students to make connections with what they have learned from the speakers with what they have read in *Witness*.

Follow Up: Be sure you and your students write thank you notes to each of your guests. At the very least, get a thank you card for each guest and have each of your students sign it (with any personal responses, if there is room).

<u>Activity 2</u>
Review the study questions and vocabulary for Assignment 3 orally together in class. Tell students that they should read Assignment 3 prior to the next class period.

LESSON NINE

Objectives

1. To read Act 3
2. To evaluate students' oral reading

Activity

Place students in a circle and read Act 3 as previously directed. As students are reading orally you may wish to complete an oral reading evaluation. A form is included on the following page for your convenience.

ORAL READING EVALUATION *Witness*

Name ______________________________ Class____________ Date ____________________

SKILL	EXCELLENT	GOOD	AVERAGE	FAIR	POOR
Fluency	5	4	3	2	1
Clarity	5	4	3	2	1
Audibility	5	4	3	2	1
Pronunciation	5	4	3	2	1
_____________	5	4	3	2	1
_____________	5	4	3	2	1

Total _____________ Grade ________________

Comments:

LESSON TEN

Objectives

1. To review main ideas, events, and vocabulary of Assignment 3
2. To help students organize the events of the story and the feelings and experiences of each character
3. To teach students about hate crimes

Activity 1

Discuss the answers to the study questions for Assingment 3 in detail as previously directed.

Activity 2

Review the vocabulary answers from the reading. Make sure students write down the correct answers.

Activity 3

Add events from the reading to character cut outs as previously directed.

Activity 4

Option 1: Provide students with a map of your area. It would be best to give them a map of your state and surrounding states. Check out a projector and laptop or take your students to a computer lab where they can visit the Southern Poverty Law Center's Intelligence Project examining active hate groups and documented hate crimes by state for the past six years (http://www.splcenter.org/intel/map/?source=redirect&url=tolerance-maps-hate). Have students mark on their maps the type of hate crime, year, and location for the past few years in your area. Once students have completed the map, ask them to write a short reaction to this assignment. Next, conduct a class discussion where you allow students to share what they learned from this assignment. Most will be surprised at the number of active hate groups in their area and will be affected by reading about the hate crimes against individuals in their area. If you have additional time, you may want to have your students visit the FBI's site with more detailed statistics about hate crimes and their victims in the United States (http://www.fbi.gov/ucr/ucr.htm).

Option 2: Select one or more national or international hate crimes that received a lot of attention. Show a video to your students or use additional educational materials found online to teach them about this specific hate crime. International suggestions include the Nazi genocide of the Jews, the ethnic cleansing in Bosnia, or the genocide in Rwanda. You could also take this time to focus on a more in-depth look at the KKK--or focus on a hate crime that may be in current events.

LESSON ELEVEN

Objectives

1. To practice writing to persuade
2. To improve students' writing abilities
3. To evaluate students' writing
4. To preview study questions and vocabulary for Assignment 4

Activity 1
Students have had a lot of exposure to hate crimes at this point in the unit and should be ready to write a persuasive essay on the subject. This persuasive essay will require students to convince someone to stop practicing hate and to become more tolerant. Distribute Writing Assignment 2 to your students and use the following rubric to provide feedback.

Activity 2
Review the study questions and vocabulary for Assignment 4 orally together in class. Tell students that they should read Assignment 4 prior to the next class period.

WRITING ASSIGNMENT #2 *Witness*

PROMPT

Leanora, Esther, and many others in the novel experience hatred from others in the town. Your assignment is to write a letter to someone who is intolerant of another group. In the letter you will persuade this person to stop practicing hate, and start being tolerant and accepting of others. The letter can be to someone you know, someone you have heard or read about, or someone in the book *Witness*.

PREWRITING

Using your notes/information from the speaker, non-fiction assignment, and other activities from class, create a list of reasons why someone should be tolerant of others. Try to include information about how hate can really damage victims physically and emotionally. You might want to include examples from the text and other personal stories you have read. You may choose to focus on a specific group of people who commonly experience hate crimes, or discuss the issue of hate in general.

DRAFTING

Write an introductory paragraph that addresses this person and his or her problem. Express your concern and begin to explain why hatred should not be a part of this person's life.

In the body paragraphs, continue to outline your reasons for wanting this person to be more tolerant and accepting of others. Remember to use your facts, statistics, and examples from the text to support your view. Make each new reason a separate paragraph.

In your concluding paragraph, make your final plea to this person. Try to end your letter with a strong story or example to leave the reader with a powerful ending.

PROMPT

When you finish the rough draft of your composition, ask a student who sits near you to read it. After reading your rough draft, he/she should tell you what he/she liked best about your work, which parts were difficult to understand, and ways in which your work could be improved. Reread your paper considering your critic's comments, and make the corrections you think are necessary. Ask your classmate what he/she thought of each of the characters/events you chose for your assignment.

PROOFREADING

Do a final proofreading of your paper double-checking your grammar, spelling, organization, and the clarity of your ideas.

LESSON TWELVE

Objectives

1. To read Act 4
2. To practice oral reading

Activity

Place students in a circle and read Act 4 as previously directed.

LESSON THIRTEEN

Objectives

1. To review main ideas, events, and vocabulary of Assignment 4
2. To help students organize the events of the story and the feelings and experiences of each character
3. To preview study questions and vocabulary for Assignment 5

Activity 1
Discuss the answers to the study questions for Assingment 4in detail as previously directed.

Activity 2
Review the vocabulary answers from the reading. Make sure students write down the correct answers.

Activity 3
Add events from the reading to character cut outs as previously described.

Activity 4
Review the study questions and vocabulary for Assignment 5 orally together in class. Tell students that they should read Assignment 5 prior to the next class period.

LESSON FOURTEEN

Objectives

1. To read Act 5
2. To practice oral reading

Activity

Place students in a circle and read Act 5 as previously directed.

LESSONS FIFTEEN AND SIXTEEN

Objectives

1. To review main ideas, events, and vocabulary of Assignment 5
2. To help students organize the events of the story and the feelings and experiences of each character
3. To discuss the novel on a deeper than direct-recall level
4. To prepare students for questions and topics covered on the test
5. To allow students to make personal connection with the text

Activity 1
Discuss the answers to the study questions for Assignment 5 in detail as previously directed.

Activity 2
Review the vocabulary answers from the reading. Make sure students write down the correct answers.

Activity 3
Add events from the reading to character cut outs as previously described.

Activity 4
Choose the questions from the Extra Discussion Questions/Writing Assignments which seem most appropriate for your students. A class discussion of these questions is most effective if students have been given the opportunity to formulate answers to the questions prior to the discussion. To this end, you may either have all the students formulate answers to all the questions, divide your class into groups and assign one or more questions to each group, or you could assign one question to each student in your class. The option you choose will make a difference in the amount of class time needed for this activity.

NOTE: Students will be asked to choose one of the Personal Response questions as a topic for their compositions in Writing Assignment #3, so either be sure to include these questions in your discussions if your students need the extra help--or be sure to skip them if you want your students to only address them in the writing assignment.

NOTE: The use of graphic organizers may be helpful to students in preparing their answers. Encourage them to use any diagrams or graphics that they feel are necessary.

EXTRA DISCUSSION QUESTIONS *Witness*

Interpretive

1. Describe the author's writing style.
2. How does the author use point of view to develop the story?
3. Under what genre does the story fall? Do you think it is closer to a play or poetry? Explain your answer.
4. What are two of the main conflicts in the story? Describe each fully.
5. What is the setting, and what does it add to the story?
6. How does the author use events from history in the novel? What does this add to the story?
7. How does the lack of capitalization add to the story?

Critical

8. What does Leanora's father mean when he asks her "how alone do you want to be, leanora? you're already nothing but a wild brown island." How is she alone? Why is it ironic that she wishes people would just leave her alone?
9. Leanora's father doesn't have a voice in the story, but the reader is still aware of several personality traits. What inferences can the reader make about Leanora's father?
10. Johnny Reeves talks about a black preacher in the south with a following of both races. He says this preacher was tried in court for inciting trouble. How was the preacher inciting trouble? Why do you think this case wasn't automatically thrown out of court?
11. Leanora compares Lewis's dying by being buried in the sandbank to the way she feels around white people. What message is she trying to convey?
12. How is Merlin Van Tornhout affected by the murder of Bobby Franks? What does he think about the two murderers?
13. Compare and contrast Sara Chickering's view of men with her view of Ira Hirsh.
14. Describe the relationship between Harvey and Viola Pettibone. How is their marriage? How well do they communicate?
15. Why does the KKK appeal to so many people? In what ways do they present themselves as decent people striving to uphold American family values?
16. When the hearse carrying the body of a slain Klansman catches fire on its way to the cemetery, people interpret that as a sign from God. Compare and contrast how Sara Chickering interprets the sign with the way Johnny Reeves does.
17. How does Leanora know to run to the train tracks? What clues led her there to save Esther?
18. What is the reason Merlin Van Tornhout gives for not saving Esther? What is the real reason he didn't?
19. Fully describe Esther's personality. What types of things interest her?
20. The judge in the Leopold and Loeb case says he doesn't believe in the death penalty for minors, saying "his decision holds with the dictates of enlightening humanity." What does this mean? What does Iris Weaver mean when she says, "enlightened humanity. now there's something the Klan could discuss at their next cross burning"?

21. The police found the body of a Polish man hanging from a tree and ruled it a suicide. What really happened to the man? What evidence is there to support another theory?
22. Who killed Jerry, Sara Chickering's dog? Why did this happen?
23. Reread the page in Act 4 when Merlin Van Tornhout is speaking about getting rat poison to pour in the Sutter's well. How does he feel about doing this job? How does Harvey feel about doing this job? Use evidence from the text to support your answer.
24. Johnny Reeves says, "there is only one way to redeem myself with my klan brothers. only one way to redeem myself with god." What does he mean by this? What literary element does this exemplify?
25. What would have happened if Esther hadn't been leaning forward to look at the crossword puzzle when her father was shot?
26. Johnny Reeves used to be one of the strongest supporters for the KKK, but is later found walking around in shock after the KKK branded his back with their letters. What does this say about the Klan and loyalty?
27. Why does Johnny Reeves commit suicide?
28. How does Esther reason that it's all right that someone tried to kill her and her father?
29. Why doesn't Esther tell Constable Johnson that she saw Johnny Reeves shoot her dad? What does she do instead?
30. In what ways does Sara act more protective over Esther after her father is shot?
31. What is the significance of "the secretary of the state of vermont has rejected the application received from the k.k.k. to do business here. good."?
32. Why didn't Merlin poison the Sutters' well?
33. Identify which characters are static and which are dynamic.
34. Why does the KKK leave Vermont?
35. How does each character grow over the course of the novel?
36. *Witness* explores the idea of hatred and how it can affect and change community. However, it is also a story of forgiveness and growth. After reading the novel, do you think it is a story teaching more about hatred or forgiveness? Explain your answer using examples from the text.

Critical/Personal Response

37. The preacher, Johnny Reeves, says, "negroes kill other negroes over gambling debts, over women, over gin." Why do you think he is blind to the same things done by white people?
38. Willie, the boy who is always teasing Leanora at school with racial comments, is son to Harvey and Viola Pettibone. Where do you think he gets his hateful attitude? How do you think his parents would react if they knew of his behavior at school? Think about your behavior at school. Would your parents be shocked if they knew how you acted sometimes?
39. Clergyman Johnny Reeves says, "we shall form a great fist, and we shall still those who oppose us. we shall strike them out, wipe them out, blot them out. together we cast those who are not like us into the arms of satan." Is this sort of statement surprising for a religious leader? Explain why or why not, using examples from your personal experiences.
40. What does Leanora hide in the hall closet the night of the cross burning? What comfort does this give her? What do you do for comfort when you are scared?

41. The KKK "appears to serve the best interest of the community, 'cleaning' it up, keeping a vigilant eye out for loose morals and lawbreakers." How does the KKK have the right to decide what moral code to follow? How do they get the power to say what is morally correct in society? How do people today decide what is morally right? Give examples of groups who try to decide for the public what is right and wrong.
42. Esther tries to stop the train so she can take her mother flowers in heaven, thinking that all dead people take the train to heaven. Why do you think her perception of how to get to heaven is so wrong? What did your parents tell you about death when you were young? How did your perceptions of death change as you got older?
43. When Clarence Darrow was pleading for the life of Leopold and Loeb he said, "why did they kill little bobby franks? not for money. not for hate. they killed him because somewhere in the infinite processes which go into the making of the boy or the man, something slipped." What do you think of this argument? Do you think this is a legitimate reason for why these two boys killed someone or is it just an excuse? Give examples to support your answer.
44. Mr. Field tells Leanora she has a lot more seeing to take in before she can sit down and rest with it. What does he mean by this? In what ways do you reflect on things you see and experience in your life?
45. Why does Ira Hirsh move to Vermont in the first place? Do you think it is worth the hassle he is getting from the KKK? What would you do in his situation?
46. Reread the passage in Act 5 by Reynard Alexander about Coolidge being elected President of the United States. What does he say about the type of election he ran? How is this election similar to or different from Presidential elections now? Do you think Coolidge's way of campaigning is better or worse than the way it is done now? Give details to support your answer.
47. Leanora says, "someone had to pay for me being a colored girl in a white world i thought. merlin ought to pay. so i waited. but then mr. field said, leanora, no way to pay a debt by stealing from someone else to do it." What did Mr. Field mean by his comment? What would you have done if you were in Leanora's situation?
48. At the end of the novel characters are given one final voice, concluding each separate story. How does each story conclude? How did you feel about the ending?

Personal Response

49. From page one the reader is confronted with "those limb-tight white girls. the ones who wouldn't dance with a negro, they went home in a huff that first day, but some came back. they told miss harvey they'd dance, but they wouldn't touch any brown skin girl." How did it feel to encounter such racism so early in the novel? How did those first few lines shape your perception of the book?
50. Some people in the story feel like joining the KKK would be easier than fighting against them. They also feel like being a part of such a large, influential group would have some advantages. Have you ever had to decide whether or not to join a group that would have some benefits, but ultimately have a negative impact? Have you seen friends or family members struggle with a decision like this? Explain your answer.
51. Sara Chickering was considering joining the KKK before Esther and Ira Hirsh came to live with her. After getting to know the two, she changed her mind about Jewish people and began to love and care for Esther and Ira as if they were her own family. Discuss a time in your life when your perceptions of a group of people changed after developing a relationship with someone from that group.

52. Reynard Alexander says, "what is the ku klux klan? is it the patriotic organization it claims to be? 100 percent americans. what is a 100 percent american? what of catholics, jews, negroes, citizens of any other race or color born here, whose fathers were born here, and grandfathers. are they not every bit as 100 percent American as the klan?" Do people today still see some people more "American" than others? How do you define an American?

53. Reynard Alexander says, "this is no longer a problem facing some other community. the klan is in our homes, our schools, our factories, and stores. it has worked its fingers through the fabric of the state and if we do not mend the rents soon, we'll fall to pieces." Give an example of a problem or situation that you didn't really believe could happen in your hometown, state, or country. How did the problem seem while it was happening somewhere else? How did it seem once it had come closer to home?

54. Reynard Alexander says, "persecution is not american. it is not american to give the power of life and death to a secret organization. it is not american to have our citizens judged by an invisible jury. it is not american to have bands of night riders apply the punishments of medieval europe to freeborn men." What do you think of his speech?

55. What would you do if you were in the situation of the Sutters or the Hirshes? How would you handle the persecution from the KKK?

56. What would you do if you were a white citizen in the town and had to watch the KKK harass your friends and neighbors?

57. Iris Weaver says, "women have waited far too long for the vote to stay out of it now." She is obviously proud of her right to vote and ready to voice her opinion in the polls. What do you think about voting? Will you vote in every election when you are old enough? Why do you think so many people choose not to vote?

58. Fitzgerald Flitt says, "there are always those who think the world is going to the dogs and that everything approached perfection only in the good old days... to those who swear our young are on the road to perdition take comfort in this--every generation has felt somewhat the same for two or three thousand years and still the world goes on." Reflect on this statement. Do you agree or disagree with what he is saying? Use examples to support your answer.

QUOTATIONS WORKSHEET *Witness*

1. no one too energetic about helping a colored man hereabouts, even if he is a neighbor.

2. no low-down white boy's gonna stop leanora sutter from getting an education.

3. the ku klux klan are here, vi. there's not a thing to stop them. we might as well join them. why not?

4. we shall form a great fist, and we shall still those who oppose us. we shall strike them out, wipe them out, blot them out...we cast those who are not like us into the arms of satan.

5. i doctor these women and i have seen over the last years a transformation in them. and what i see, the opening of roses kept bud-tight so many years, it warms the aging soul.

6. he said we'd all be better off if we got the family out of the restaurant and back to the dinner table. he said the average woman, she loves her home and family first. she might have got distracted when she was earning wages while her man fought in the great war. but the trend is the other way now.

7. ...the flames spread from the base to the top. in a matter of minutes the cross arm pulsed with fire. the flames leaping, seeking heaven, neighbor, the white crucifix scoring the night blazed perfect.

8. klan can seem mighty right-minded, with their talk of family virtue, might decent, if you don't scratch the surface.

9. ...i declared the klan a movement of god.

10. whoever wrote that letter said they saw the article about leanora saving the hirsh child from the train. said, they'd tie them both to the tracks next time, make sure neither walked away.

11. what is the ku klux klan? is it the patriotic organization it claims to be?... what of catholics, jews, negroes, citizens of any other race or color born here, whose fathers were born here, and grandfathers. are they not every bit as 100 percent american as the klan?

12. 'why did they kill little bobby franks? not for money. not for hate. they killed him because somewhere in the infinite processes which go into the making of the boy or the man, something slipped.' ...something has slipped and as a result we are all sliding back toward the dark ages.

13. this is no longer a problem facing some other community. the klan is in our homes, our schools, our factories, and stores. it has worked its fingers through the fabric of the state and if we do not mend the rents soon, we'll fall to pieces.

14. we threw johnny reeves out of the klan. imagine a grown man a preacher forcing himself on a child.

15. in private, harvey pettibone handed me rat poison from his store. pour it in sutter's well, he said.

16. there is only one way to redeem myself with my klan brother. only one way to redeem myself with god.

17. i never thought it'd come to this. thought i'd be helping the law, not breaking it.

18. how grateful i am that she was leaning forward over mr. hirsh's crossword puzzle. if not she would have taken the bullet herself, straight through, and she wouldn't be alive now,...

19. persecution is not american. it is not american to give the power of life and death to a secret organization. it is not american to have our citizens judged by a invisible jury. it is not american to have bands of night riders apply the punishments of medieval europe to freeborn men.

20. we have antilynching laws on the books. but that isn't why necks are less often swinging in nooses. it is the people saying no.

21. it didn't matter that someone didn't like us so much that they did take a gun to kill us because so many people did like us and did come to sara chickering's house to help us.

22. ...even if i did not tell constable johnson what i did see, i can tell God that i saw johnny reeves that night daddy did get a bullet through him. and i did think if i tell God in johnny reeves' own church, God does know what to do.

23. women have waited far too long for the vote to stay out of it now. but i'll vote for the man i choose. i don't need anyone, not even senator greene, telling me what to think.

24. if i had done what the klan sent me out to do, i'd be in jail a long time. but i didn't. i couldn't...and she was still a colored girl but she wasn't just a colored girl, and i couldn't poison her well, so i ran.

25. a long time ago i wrote miss helen keller about how maybe we'd be better off if no one could see. then nobody would mind about a person's skin color.

26. i keep looking over my shoulder since constable johnson let me come home. but the hoods and robes have vanished from vermont.

27. there are always those who think the world is going to the dogs and that everthing approached perfection only in the good old days...to those who swear our young are on the road to perdition take comfort in this--every generation has felt somewhat the same for two or three thousand years and still the world goes on.

28. someone had to pay for me being a colored girl in a white world i thought. merlin ought to pay. so i waited. but then mr. feld said, leanora, no way to pay a debt by stealing from someone else to do it.

LESSON SEVENTEEN

Objectives

1. To practice expressing personal opinions in writing using a topic from *Witness*
2. To improve students' writing abilities
3. To evaluate students' writing
4. To think through ideas presented in *Witness*

Activity

Distribute Writing Assignment 3 and discuss the assignment in detail.

Use the attached rubric to give feedback to your students.

NOTE: As students complete this writing assignment, you may want to call individuals up for writing conferences about the past two writing assignments. Use the evaluation form to guide you in your conference.

WRITING ASSIGNMENT #3 *Witness*

PROMPT

There are many interesting points and ideas brought up in the book *Witness*. Your assignment is to choose one of the Personal Response questions from the Extra Discussion Questions and write a composition giving your opinion(s) about the topic presented. If you feel strongly about a topic presented in the book that is not an option in the Personal Response questions, compose a question and ask permission to write about that.

PREWRITING

Look at the questions carefully and decide which one to choose. Think about the question and make notes about your thoughts. Jot down words, phrases, ideas, images, and things from the book that come to mind about that topic.

DRAFTING

This composition should be written in first person. It will have an introductory paragraph where you will introduce your topic and your opinion about it.

The body of your composition should include several paragraphs providing support for your opinions. You will want to give multiple examples, providing support from materials in this unit and experiences in your own life.

Your composition should have a conclusion that contains a final summary of your views on the topic. You may want to leave a lasting impression on your reader with a powerful example or final point.

PROMPT

When you finish the rough draft of your composition, ask a student who sits near you to read it. After reading your rough draft, he/she should tell you what he/she liked best about your work, which parts were difficult to understand, and ways in which your work could be improved. Reread your paper considering your critic's comments, and make the corrections you think are necessary.

PROOFREADING

Do a final proofreading of your paper double-checking your grammar, spelling, organization, and the clarity of your ideas.

WRITING EVALUATION FORM - *Witness*

Name ______________________________ Date ________________________

Writing Assignment # _______ Grade _________________

Circle One For Each Item:

Introduction:	excellent	good	fair	poor
Body Paragraphs:	excellent	good	fair	poor
Conclusion:	excellent	good	fair	poor
Grammar:	excellent	good	fair	poor
Spelling:	excellent	good	fair	poor
Punctuation:	excellent	good	fair	poor
Legibility:	excellent	good	fair	poor
Persuasiveness:	excellent	good	fair	poor
_____________	excellent	good	fair	poor

Strengths:

Weaknesses:

Comments/Suggestions:

LESSON EIGHTEEN

Objectives

1. To review and evaluate students' unit projects
2. To practice speaking and presentation skills
3. To generate class discussion about the unit
4. To connect ideas from the novel with events in students' lives
5. To evaluate students' reaction to the unit

Activity 1

Have students present their projects to the class. Ask students to display their projects and share some of their facts they found in their research. If at all possible, allow for discussion of these facts and statistics during presentations. Encourage students to think about the research they did and how it relates to their lives.

Activity 2

Give students the *Witness* Unit Reaction sheet. Give them a chance to answer the questions and give feedback about the unit. Read over the feedback and make any necessary adjustments to the unit before you begin to teach it the following year.

UNIT REACTION *Witness*

1. What were your overall impressions of *Witness*?

2. How likely are you to read one of Karen Hesse's other books?

3. How likely are you to read other young adult historical fiction books?

4. What was your favorite assignment in the unit? Why?

5. What was your least favorite assignment in the unit? Why?

6. What was most helpful to you in this unit?

7. What assignment do you think should be changed? Why?

8. What was something that surprised you about your topic while doing research?

9. How did the research and information in the projects presented affect you?

10. How has this book and project affected your life (the decisions you make, how you view others, etc)?

Use the space below to write any other comments you have regarding this unit:

LESSON NINETEEN

Objectives

1. To review all of the vocabulary work done in this unit
2. To allow students to practice writing a letter
3. To allow students to show the author their appreciation for the book

Activity 1

Choose one (or more) of the vocabulary review activities listed below and spend your class period as directed in the activity. Some of the materials for these review activities are located in the Vocabulary Resource Materials section in this LitPlan.

VOCABULARY REVIEW ACTIVITIES

1. Divide your class into two teams and have an old-fashioned spelling or definition bee.

2. Give each of your students (or students in groups of two, three or four) a *Witness* Vocabulary Word Search Puzzle. The person (group) to find all of the vocabulary words in the puzzle first wins.

3. Give students a *Witness* Vocabulary Word Search Puzzle without the word list. The person or group to find the most vocabulary words in the puzzle wins.

4. Use a *Witness* Vocabulary Crossword Puzzle. Put the puzzle onto a transparency on the overhead projector (so everyone can see it), and do the puzzle together as a class.

5. Give students a *Witness* Vocabulary Matching Worksheet to do.

6. Divide your class into two teams. Use *Witness* vocabulary words with their letters jumbled as a word list. Student 1 from Team A faces off against Student 1 from Team B. You write the first jumbled word on the board. The first student (1A or 1B) to unscramble the word wins the chance for his/her team to score points. If 1A wins the jumble, go to student 2A and give him/her a definition. He/she must give you the correct spelling of the vocabulary word which fits that definition. If he/she does, Team A scores a point, and you give student 3A a definition for which you expect a correctly spelled matching vocabulary word. Continue giving Team A definitions until some team member makes an incorrect response. An incorrect response sends the game back to the jumbled-word face off, this time with students 2A and 2B. Instead of repeating giving definitions to the first few students of each team, continue with the student after the one who gave the last incorrect response on the team. For example, if Team B wins the jumbled-word face-off, and student 5B gave the last incorrect answer for Team B, you would start this round of definition questions with student 6B, and so on. The team with the most points wins!

7. Have students write a story in which they correctly use as many vocabulary words as possible. Have students read their compositions orally! Post the most original compositions on your bulletin board!

Activity 2

Give students the Letter to the Author assignment sheet. If needed, review how to write a formal letter with your students. Give them the remainder of the class time to complete the letter. Once you have proofread all the letters and students have had the chance to correct any mistakes, mail the letters to Karen Hesse at:

—

Karen Hesse
c/o Scholastic, Inc.
557 Broadway
New York, NY 10012-3999

NOTE: This assignment may be used as an extra credit opportunity. You may offer extra credit for simply writing the letter, or offer extra credit for those who type their letter.

LETTER TO THE AUTHOR

Often times, books are written to make people think about serious issues. Think about the point the author was trying to make in writing this book. Then, compose a letter to the author expressing how this book has affected your life.

Topics to include in your letter:

- What you liked about the book
- How you could relate to this book
- How realistic the book was
- What you learned from the book
- What issues the book made you think about
- How you felt when reading the book
- How you have changed since reading the book
- Anything else you think the author should know

Necessary Elements:

- Your letter must by typed
- You should begin your letter by saying Dear Ms. ___________________,
- You should have an introductory paragraph where you introduce yourself
- You should have body paragraphs
- You should have a friendly conclusion to the letter
- Underneath your signature you should include your home address and email address in case the author wishes to write you back

Remember to **proofread this letter**.

Most authors enjoy receiving letters from readers and like to see how their hard work has affected others. Some authors even respond to letters from their readers, so don't be surprised if you get a reply.

LESSON TWENTY

Objectives
To review the main ideas and events in *Witness*

Activity
Choose one of the review games/activities suggested in this unit and spend your class time as directed there.

REVIEW GAMES/ACTIVITIES *Witness*

1. Ask the class to make up a unit test for *Witness.* The test should have 4 sections: matching, true/false, short answer, and essay. Students may use 1/2 period to make the test and then swap papers and use the other 1/2 class period to take a test a classmate has devised (open book). You may want to use the unit test included in this packet or take questions from the students' unit tests to formulate your own test.

2. Take 1/2 period for students to make up true and false questions (including the answers). Collect the papers and divide the class into two teams. Draw a big tic-tac-toe board on the chalk board. Make one team X and one team O. Ask questions to each side, giving each student one turn. If the question is answered correctly, that students' team's letter (X or O) is placed in the box. If the answer is incorrect, no letter is placed in the box. The object is to get three in a row like tic-tac-toe. You may want to keep track of the number of games won for each team.

3. Take 1/2 period for students to make up questions (true/false and short answer). Collect the questions. Divide the class into two teams. You'll alternate asking questions to individual members of teams A & B (like in a spelling bee). The question keeps going from A to B until it is correctly answered, then a new question is asked. A correct answer does not allow the team to get another question. Correct answers are +2 points; incorrect answers are -1 point.

4. Have students pair up and quiz each other from their study guides and class notes.

5. Give students a *Witness* crossword puzzle to complete.

6. Play What's My Line?. This is similar to the old television show. Students assume the roles of different characters from the epic. One student gives clues to the class, or to a panel of contestants. The contestants try to guess the identity of the guest. Students may enjoy assisting you in creating rules and procedures for the game.

7. Divide your class into two teams. Use *Witness* crossword words with their letters jumbled as a word list. Student 1 from Team A faces off against Student 1 from Team B. You write the first jumbled word on the board. The first student (1A or 1B) to unscramble the word wins the chance for his/her team to score points. If 1A wins the jumble, go to student 2A and give him/her a clue. He/she must give you the correct word which matches that clue. If he/she does, Team A scores a point, and you give student 3A a clue for which you expect another correct response. Continue giving Team A clues until some team member makes an incorrect response. An incorrect response sends the game back to the jumbled-word face off, this time with students 2A and 2B. Instead of repeating giving clues to the first few students of each team, continue with the student after the one who gave the last incorrect response on the team. For example, if Team B wins the jumbled-word face-off, and student 5B gave the last incorrect answer for Team B, you would start this round of clue questions with student 6B, and so on. The team with the most points wins!

8. Play Jeopardy. Divide the class into two groups. Assign each group a category or book from the epic and have them devise answers for that category. Play the game according to the television show procedures.

9. Play Drawing in the Details. This is similar to Pictionary. Divide students into teams. A student from one team draws a scene from the epic. (You may want to specify the Book or section.) Drawings should be kept simple, to keep the pace lively. Students in the opposing team locate the scene in their books and read it aloud. If they are incorrect, the illustrator's team has a chance to guess. Involve students in setting up a scoring system and any other necessary rules.

LESSON TWENTY ONE

Objectives
To test the students' understanding of the main ideas and themes in *Witness*

Activity 1
Distribute the unit tests, give students ample time to complete them, and collect the tests when students finish. Remember to collect assigned books prior to the end of the class period.

NOTES ABOUT THE UNIT TESTS IN THIS UNIT:

NOTE: There are 5 different unit tests included in the LitPlan Teacher Pack. Two are short answer, two are multiple choice. There is one advanced short answer test. The answers to the advanced short answer test will be based on the discussions you have had during class and should be graded accordingly. You should choose the tests and/or test parts which best suit your needs. Matching and short answer tests have answer keys. For essay type questions, grade according to your own criteria based on class discussions and the level of your students. Also, you will need to choose vocabulary words to read orally for the vocabulary section of the short answer tests.

Activity 2
Collect all test papers and assigned books prior to the end of the class period.

UNIT TESTS

Witness SHORT ANSWER UNIT TEST 1

I. MATCHING/IDENTIFY

____	1.	VIOLA	A.	Owns a shoe store in town
____	2.	LEOPOLD	B.	Helps save Ira Hirsh
____	3.	IRA	C.	______ and Loeb kill a teenage boy in Chicago.
____	4.	MERLIN	D.	Wants to be married in KKK robes
____	5.	IRIS	E.	She is like a mother to Esther.
____	6.	REYNARD	F.	Tries to rescue his girlfriend from the orphanage
____	7.	ESTHER	G.	Hassles Leanora about her race
____	8.	JOHNNY	H.	Saw the person who shot Ira Hirsh
____	9.	MARY	I.	Does not approve of her husband's involvement with the Klan
____	10.	PERCELLE	J.	She was stuck in a wagon in the cold for too long and later died: Mrs. _____.
____	11.	SARA	K.	Is a bootlegger on the side to earn extra money
____	12.	FITZGERALD	L.	He gives Merlin the keys to his business.
____	13.	HARVEY	M.	Rich, white boy who was murdered
____	14.	FIELD	N.	Leanora gets a signed book from her.
____	15.	SUTTER	O.	Sara's dog that is killed by the Klan
____	16.	PETTIBONE	P.	Shot Ira Hirsh
____	17.	FRANKS	Q.	Person in charge of maintaining peace in the town
____	18.	JERRY	R.	Clears Merlin's name
____	19.	KELLER	S.	____ begins to have doubts about the Klan when they get more violent.
____	20.	LEANORA	T.	Leanora helps him and they become friends.

II. SHORT ANSWER

1. How do Harvey and Viola Pettibone feel about the Ku Klux Klan?

2. Mr. Field offers Leanora gifts that she would love to have. Each time he offers her something she wants, she declines his offer. Why doesn't she take his gifts when she wants them so much?

3. What groups does the KKK target?

4. What does the KKK do to keep up the appearance that they are serving the community?

5. Why does Esther stand on the railroad tracks and refuse to move as a train approaches?

6. What happens to Merlin Van Tornhout when he picks up a fellow Klansman on the way to a KKK meeting?

7. What is Leanora's relationship with Mr. Field?

8. What happens to Ira Hirsh?

9. Why does Merlin Van Tornhout run away?

10. Who saw the person who shot Ira Hirsh?

III. ESSAY

1. Why did the author choose to write a story from 11 different points of view? How did this affect the novel and its themes?

2. At the end of the novel, how has the two changed as a result of the Klan's presence?

IV. Vocabulary

A. Write the vocabulary words you are given. After writing them down, go back and write in their definitions.

Word	Definition
1	
2	
3	
4	
5	
6	
7	
8	
9	
10	

Witness SHORT ANSWER UNIT TEST 1 Answer Key

I. MATCHING/IDENTIFY

I	1. VIOLA	A.	Owns a shoe store in town
C	2. LEOPOLD	B.	Helps save Ira Hirsh
A	3. IRA	C.	______ and Loeb kill a teenage boy in Chicago.
F	4. MERLIN	D.	Wants to be married in KKK robes
K	5. IRIS	E.	She is like a mother to Esther.
L	6. REYNARD	F.	Tries to rescue his girlfriend from the orphanage
H	7. ESTHER	G.	Hassles Leanora about her race
P	8. JOHNNY	H.	Saw the person who shot Ira Hirsh
D	9. MARY	I.	Does not approve of her husband's involvement with the Klan
Q	10. PERCELLE	J.	She was stuck in a wagon in the cold for too long and later died: Mrs. _____.
E	11. SARA	K.	Is a bootlegger on the side to earn extra money
B	12. FITZGERALD	L.	He gives Merlin the keys to his business.
S	13. HARVEY	M.	Rich, white boy who was murdered
T	14. FIELD	N.	Leanora gets a signed book from her.
J	15. SUTTER	O.	Sara's dog that is killed by the Klan
G	16. PETTIBONE	P.	Shot Ira Hirsh
M	17. FRANKS	Q.	Person in charge of maintaining peace in the town
O	18. JERRY	R.	Clears Merlin's name
N	19. KELLER	S.	____ begins to have doubts about the Klan when they get more violent.
R	20. LEANORA	T.	Leanora helps him and they become friends.

II. SHORT ANSWER

1. How do Harvey and Viola Pettibone feel about the Ku Klux Klan?
   Harvey wants to join the KKK, but his wife, Viola, is against the idea of being a member of such a violent group.
2. Mr. Field offers Leanora gifts that she would love to have. Each time he offers her something she wants, she declines his offer. Why doesn't she take his gifts when she wants them so much?
   She knows that if she walks from Mr. Field's neighborhood to her neighborhood with something expensive, everyone would assume she stole it. She doesn't think having the gift is worth the trouble it would probably bring.
3. What groups does the KKK target?
   The KKK targets Catholics, Jewish people, and black people with their hate.
4. What does the KKK do to keep up the appearance that they are serving the community?
   They deliver baskets to the needy and give money to the poor.
5. Why does Esther stand on the railroad tracks and refuse to move as a train approaches?
   She was told her mother took a train to heaven. She thinks that all people who die get to heaven by train, and she wants to stop the train so she can get on and take her mother some flowers in heaven.
6. What happens to Merlin Van Tornhout when he picks up a fellow Klansman on the way to a KKK meeting?
   The man gets in the car and pulls out a knife, making Merlin get out so he can have his car.
7. What is Leanora's relationship with Mr. Field?
   She becomes friends with him and enjoys listening to him talk.
8. What happens to Ira Hirsh?
   He is shot while he is sitting at the kitchen table with Esther on his lap.
9. Why does Merlin Van Tornhout run away?
   Harvey tells him that if he couldn't put the rat poison in the Sutters' well, then he better run because the Klan would come after him.
10. Who saw the person who shot Ira Hirsh?
    Esther saw the man who shot her father.

IV. Vocabulary

Write the vocabulary words and definitions you will use for this test.

Word	Definition
1	
2	
3	
4	
5	
6	
7	
8	
9	
10	

Witness SHORT ANSWER UNIT TEST 2

I. MATCHING/IDENTIFY

____ 1.	LEOPOLD	A.	Leanora gets a signed book from her.
____ 2.	IRA	B.	Klan thinks this family is worse than the Sutters.
____ 3.	MERLIN	C.	Sara's dog that is killed by the Klan
____ 4.	IRIS	D.	She was stuck in a wagon in the cold for too long and later died: Mrs. _____.
____ 5.	REYNARD	E.	Is a bootlegger on the side to earn extra money
____ 6.	ESTHER	F.	Leanora helps him and they become friends.
____ 7.	JOHNNY	G.	Clears Merlin's name
____ 8.	MARY	H.	Person in charge of maintaining peace in the town
____ 9.	PERCELLE	I.	______ and Loeb kill a teenage boy in Chicago.
____ 10.	SARA	J.	Rich, white boy who was murdered
____ 11.	FITZGERALD	K.	Was kicked out of the KKK
____ 12.	HARVEY	L.	Wants to be married in KKK robes
____ 13.	FIELD	M.	Helps save Ira Hirsh
____ 14.	SUTTER	N.	Tries to rescue his girlfriend from the orphanage
____ 15.	FRANKS	O.	Saw the person who shot Ira Hirsh
____ 16.	JERRY	P.	She is like a mother to Esther.
____ 17.	REEVES	Q.	He gives Merlin the keys to his business.
____ 18.	HIRSH	R.	Shot Ira Hirsh
____ 19.	KELLER	S.	____ begins to have doubts about the Klan when they get more violent.
____ 20.	LEANORA	T.	Owns a shoe store in town

II. SHORT ANSWER

1. What groups does the KKK target?

2. Why does Ira Hirsh consider moving out of Sara Chickering's house?

3. Why does Esther stand on the railroad tracks and refuse to move as a train approaches?

4. What could Merlin Van Tornhout do to advance in the KKK?

5. What is Leanora's relationship with Mr. Field?

6. Why does Johnny Reeves get kicked out of the KKK?

7. What does the KKK want Merlin Van Tornhout to do?

8. What happens to Ira Hirsh?

9. Why does Merlin Van Tornhout run away?

10. Who clears Merlin's name and provides evidence that he did not shoot Ira Hirsh?

III. ESSAY

1. How does each character grow over the course of the novel?

2. Why did the author choose to write a story from 11 different points of view? How did this affect the novel and its themes?

IV. Vocabulary

A. Write the vocabulary words you are given. After writing them down, go back and write in their definitions.

Word	Definition
1	
2	
3	
4	
5	
6	
7	
8	
9	
10	

Witness SHORT ANSWER UNIT TEST 2 Answer Key

I. MATCHING/IDENTIFY

I	1. LEOPOLD	A. Leanora gets a signed book from her.
T	2. IRA	B. Klan thinks this family is worse than the Sutters.
N	3. MERLIN	C. Sara's dog that is killed by the Klan
E	4. IRIS	D. She was stuck in a wagon in the cold for too long and later died: Mrs. _____.
Q	5. REYNARD	E. Is a bootlegger on the side to earn extra money
O	6. ESTHER	F. Leanora helps him and they become friends.
R	7. JOHNNY	G. Clears Merlin's name
L	8. MARY	H. Person in charge of maintaining peace in the town
H	9. PERCELLE	I. ______ and Loeb kill a teenage boy in Chicago.
P	10. SARA	J. Rich, white boy who was murdered
M	11. FITZGERALD	K. Was kicked out of the KKK
S	12. HARVEY	L. Wants to be married in KKK robes
F	13. FIELD	M. Helps save Ira Hirsh
D	14. SUTTER	N. Tries to rescue his girlfriend from the orphanage
J	15. FRANKS	O. Saw the person who shot Ira Hirsh
C	16. JERRY	P. She is like a mother to Esther.
K	17. REEVES	Q. He gives Merlin the keys to his business.
B	18. HIRSH	R. Shot Ira Hirsh
A	19. KELLER	S. ____ begins to have doubts about the Klan when they get more violent.
G	20. LEANORA	T. Owns a shoe store in town

II. SHORT ANSWER

1. What groups does the KKK target?
   The KKK targets Catholics, Jewish people, and black people with their hate.
2. Why does Ira Hirsh consider moving out of Sara Chickering's house?
   Someone throws a rock through Sara's window with a note attached. He wants to move out of the house so that the KKK will leave Sara alone.
3. Why does Esther stand on the railroad tracks and refuse to move as a train approaches?
   She was told her mother took a train to heaven. She thinks that all people who die get to heaven by train, and she wants to stop the train so she can get on and take her mother some flowers in heaven.
4. What could Merlin Van Tornhout do to advance in the KKK?
   He could give them the keys to the newspaper since he works there and has access to everything.
5. What is Leanora's relationship with Mr. Field?
   She becomes friends with him and enjoys listening to him talk.
6. Why does Johnny Reeves get kicked out of the KKK?
   His mother gives Harvey a letter saying she caught him in an inappropriate situation with a young school girl. The KKK won't tolerate that type of behavior, so he is kicked out.
7. What does the KKK want Merlin Van Tornhout to do?
   They want him to put rat poison in the Sutters' well.
8. What happens to Ira Hirsh?
   He is shot while he is sitting at the kitchen table with Esther on his lap.
9. Why does Merlin Van Tornhout run away?
   Harvey tells him that if he couldn't put the rat poison in the Sutters' well, then he better run because the Klan would come after him.
10. Who clears Merlin's name and provides evidence that he did not shoot Ira Hirsh?
    Leanora confesses that Merlin did not do the crime and provides evidence that he is innocent.

IV. Vocabulary

Write the vocabulary words and definitions you will use for this test.

Word	Definition
1	
2	
3	
4	
5	
6	
7	
8	
9	
10	

Witness ADVANCED SHORT ANSWER UNIT TEST

I. MATCHING/IDENTIFY

____	1.	IRA	A.	Helps save Ira Hirsh
____	2.	IRIS	B.	Was suffocated by a sandbank cave-in
____	3.	REYNARD	C.	Person in charge of maintaining peace in the town
____	4.	ESTHER	D.	Is a bootlegger on the side to earn extra money
____	5.	JOHNNY	E.	She was stuck in a wagon in the cold for too long and later died: Mrs. _____.
____	6.	MARY	F.	Hassles Leanora about her race
____	7.	PERCELLE	G.	Wants to be married in KKK robes
____	8.	SARA	H.	Rich, white boy who was murdered
____	9.	FITZGERALD	I.	Owns a shoe store in town
____	10.	HARVEY	J.	Leanora gets a signed book from her.
____	11.	FIELD	K.	Saw the person who shot Ira Hirsh
____	12.	SUTTER	L.	Klan thinks this family is worse than the Sutters.
____	13.	PETTIBONE	M.	____ begins to have doubts about the Klan when they get more violent.
____	14.	LEWIS	N.	Sara's dog that is killed by the Klan
____	15.	FRANKS	O.	Clears Merlin's name
____	16.	JERRY	P.	Shot Ira Hirsh
____	17.	REEVES	Q.	She is like a mother to Esther.
____	18.	HIRSH	R.	Was kicked out of the KKK
____	19.	KELLER	S.	He gives Merlin the keys to his business.
____	20.	LEANORA	T.	Leanora helps him and they become friends.

II. SHORT ANSWER

1. Why does the KKK appeal to so many people? In what ways do they present themselves as decent people striving to uphold American family values?

2. Why doesn't Esther tell Constable Johnson that she saw Johnny Reeves shoot her dad? What does she do instead?

3. What is the significance of "the secretary of the state of vermont has rejected the application received from the k.k.k. to do business here. good."?

4. Why did the author choose to write a story from 11 different points of view? How did this affect the novel and its themes?

5. At the end of the novel, how has the two changed as a result of the Klan's presence?

6. Compare and contrast how Merlin and Harvey feel about pouring rat poison in the Sutters' well. Use evidence for the text to support your answer.

III. ESSAY

1. *Witness* explores the idea of hatred and how it can affect and change community. However, it is also a story of forgiveness and growth. After reading the novel, do you think it is a story teaching more about hatred or forgiveness? Explain your answer using examples from the text.

IV. Vocabulary

A. Write the vocabulary words you are given. After writing them down, go back and write in their definitions.

Word	Definition
1	
2	
3	
4	
5	
6	
7	
8	
9	
10	

B. Write a paragraph about the book using 8 of the 10 vocabulary words above.

Witness ADVANCED SHORT ANSWER UNIT TEST Answer Key

I. MATCHING/IDENTIFY

I	1. IRA	A. Helps save Ira Hirsh
D	2. IRIS	B. Was suffocated by a sandbank cave-in
S	3. REYNARD	C. Person in charge of maintaining peace in the town
K	4. ESTHER	D. Is a bootlegger on the side to earn extra money
P	5. JOHNNY	E. She was stuck in a wagon in the cold for too long and later died: Mrs. _____.
G	6. MARY	F. Hassles Leanora about her race
C	7. PERCELLE	G. Wants to be married in KKK robes
Q	8. SARA	H. Rich, white boy who was murdered
A	9. FITZGERALD	I. Owns a shoe store in town
M	10. HARVEY	J. Leanora gets a signed book from her.
T	11. FIELD	K. Saw the person who shot Ira Hirsh
E	12. SUTTER	L. Klan thinks this family is worse than the Sutters.
F	13. PETTIBONE	M. ____ begins to have doubts about the Klan when they get more violent.
B	14. LEWIS	N. Sara's dog that is killed by the Klan
H	15. FRANKS	O. Clears Merlin's name
N	16. JERRY	P. Shot Ira Hirsh
R	17. REEVES	Q. She is like a mother to Esther.
L	18. HIRSH	R. Was kicked out of the KKK
J	19. KELLER	S. He gives Merlin the keys to his business.
O	20. LEANORA	T. Leanora helps him and they become friends.

IV. Vocabulary

Write the vocabulary words and definitions you will use for this test.

Word	Definition
1	
2	
3	
4	
5	
6	
7	
8	
9	
10	

Witness MULTIPLE CHOICE UNIT TEST 1

I. MATCHING/IDENTIFY

____ 1.	VIOLA	A.	She was stuck in a wagon in the cold for too long and later died: Mrs. _____.
____ 2.	LEOPOLD	B.	He gives Merlin the keys to his business.
____ 3.	IRA	C.	Hassles Leanora about her race
____ 4.	MERLIN	D.	______ and Loeb kill a teenage boy in Chicago.
____ 5.	IRIS	E.	She is like a mother to Esther.
____ 6.	REYNARD	F.	Klan thinks this family is worse than the Sutters.
____ 7.	ESTHER	G.	Was suffocated by a sandbank cave-in
____ 8.	JOHNNY	H.	Owns a shoe store in town
____ 9.	MARY	I.	____ begins to have doubts about the Klan when they get more violent.
____ 10.	PERCELLE	J.	Person in charge of maintaining peace in the town
____ 11.	SARA	K.	Wants to be married in KKK robes
____ 12.	FITZGERALD	L.	Helps save Ira Hirsh
____ 13.	HARVEY	M.	Clears Merlin's name
____ 14.	FIELD	N.	Does not approve of her husband's involvement with the Klan
____ 15.	SUTTER	O.	Sara's dog that is killed by the Klan
____ 16.	PETTIBONE	P.	Saw the person who shot Ira Hirsh
____ 17.	LEWIS	Q.	Leanora helps him and they become friends.
____ 18.	JERRY	R.	Is a bootlegger on the side to earn extra money
____ 19.	HIRSH	S.	Shot Ira Hirsh
____ 20.	LEANORA	T.	Tries to rescue his girlfriend from the orphanage

II. MULTIPLE CHOICE

1. How do Harvey and Viola Pettibone feel about the Ku Klux Klan?
   A. They both want to join.
   B. Viola wants to join and Harvey doesn't.
   C. They are both against joining.
   D. Harvey wants to join and Viola doesn't.

2. What is Leanora's relationship with Mr. Field?
   A. She becomes friends with him and enjoys listening to him talk.
   B. She starts to look at him as more of a father than her real dad.
   C. She gets bored with all his rambling and wishes he would hurry and get better.
   D. She begins to hate him since he obviously doesn't like black people.

3. What happens to Ira Hirsh?
   A. He is severely beaten.
   B. He is hanged.
   C. He is tarred and feathered.
   D. He is shot.

4. Why does Merlin Van Tornhout run away?
   A. He is tired of being a part of the Klan and wants out. He knows he wouldn't be able to just quit, so he runs away.
   B. He can't follow through with what the Klan wants him to do, so Harvey tells him to leave town before the Klan comes after him.
   C. His father is beating him, and he can't take it anymore.
   D. He runs away to be with his girlfriend, Mary. The two work out a plan to get married without anyone knowing.

5. What does the KKK do to keep up the appearance that they are serving the community?
   A. They help the church raise money for the poor.
   B. All the members attend church regularly.
   C. They deliver baskets the needy and give money to the poor.
   D. They buy clothes and school supplies for kids who come from poor families.

6. Why does Esther stand on the railroad tracks and refuse to move as a train approaches?
   A. She was told her mother took a train to heaven. She thinks that all people who die get to heaven by train, and she wants to stop the train so she can get on and take her mother some flowers in heaven.
   B. She misses her friends and family in New York but doesn't have enough money to visit them. She stands on the tracks hoping the train conductor will feel bad for her and let her go to New York for free.
   C. She finds a litter of baby kittens on the train tracks and is trying to save them. As the train approaches, she stands in the way to stop it before it hits the kittens.
   D. She enjoys the circus animals so much she wants to see them one last time before they leave town. The animals have been loaded on the train, and she tries to stop it.

7. What happens to Merlin Van Tornhout when he picks up a fellow Klansman on the way to a KKK meeting?
   A. The man pulls out a knife and steals Merlin's car.
   B. The man agrees to help Merlin get his girlfriend out of the orphanage.
   C. The man tells Merlin he will help get him promoted to a higher positon in the KKK.
   D. The man beats up Merlin and steals his wallet.

8. Mr. Field offers Leanora gifts that she would love to have. Each time he offers her something she wants, she declines his offer. Why doesn't she take his gifts when she wants them so much?
   A. By taking the gifts she would feel obligated to continue working for him at a time when she is hoping to stop soon.
   B. She is worried people will think she is stealing the items from him.
   C. Her father won't let her take handouts from others. He thinks they are doing just fine on their own.
   D. She thinks it is improper for a black girl to take gifts from a white man.

9. What groups does the KKK target?
   A. Protestants, black people, and poor people
   B. Catholics, poor people, and black people
   C. Catholics, black people, and Jewish people
   D. Protestants, black people, and foreigners

10. Who saw the person who shot Ira Hirsh?
   A. Esther Hirsh
   B. Iris Weaver
   C. Harvey Pettibone
   D. Leanora Sutter

III. ESSAY

1. Why did the author choose to write a story from 11 different points of view? How did this affect the novel and its themes?

2. At the end of the novel, how has the two changed as a result of the Klan's presence?

IV. VOCABULARY

____ 1.	INCITING	A.	Misleading; to make others believe something that is not true
____ 2.	INORDINATE	B.	Tame; gentle; kind
____ 3.	ENDURE	C.	Firm; strong; having endurance
____ 4.	FIERCE	D.	Punishment or harassment usually of a severe nature on the basis of race, religion, or political opinion
____ 5.	WIELD	E.	Very impressive because of great size, stately appearance, or dignity
____ 6.	DECEPTIVE	F.	Reprimand or criticize harshly and usually angrily
____ 7.	VIGILANT	G.	Carry on despite hardships
____ 8.	UNSCRUPULOUS	H.	Looked intently, searchingly, or with difficulty
____ 9.	PINNACLE	I.	Exceeding reasonable limits; uncontrolled
____ 10.	SCOLD	J.	Future state of the wicked; damnation; hell
____ 11.	VEXED	K.	Conflict; struggle; clash
____ 12.	STOUT	L.	Exercise power, or influence as in ruling or dominating
____ 13.	RATTLED	M.	Stirring up, encouraging or prompting into action
____ 14.	PERSECUTION	N.	Without principles
____ 15.	ENTWINED	O.	Furiously intense; wild; violent in force
____ 16.	PEERED	P.	Around or twisted together
____ 17.	STRIFE	Q.	Flustered; unnerved; confused
____ 18.	MEEK	R.	The highest point, as with success, power, or fame
____ 19.	IMPOSING	S.	Irritated; annoyed
____ 20.	PERDITION	T.	On the alert; watchful

Witness MULTIPLE CHOICE UNIT TEST 1 Answer Key

I. MATCHING/IDENTIFY

N	1. VIOLA	A. She was stuck in a wagon in the cold for too long and later died: Mrs. _____.
D	2. LEOPOLD	B. He gives Merlin the keys to his business.
H	3. IRA	C. Hassles Leanora about her race
T	4. MERLIN	D. ______ and Loeb kill a teenage boy in Chicago.
R	5. IRIS	E. She is like a mother to Esther.
B	6. REYNARD	F. Klan thinks this family is worse than the Sutters.
P	7. ESTHER	G. Was suffocated by a sandbank cave-in
S	8. JOHNNY	H. Owns a shoe store in town
K	9. MARY	I. ____ begins to have doubts about the Klan when they get more violent.
J	10. PERCELLE	J. Person in charge of maintaining peace in the town
E	11. SARA	K. Wants to be married in KKK robes
L	12. FITZGERALD	L. Helps save Ira Hirsh
I	13. HARVEY	M. Clears Merlin's name
Q	14. FIELD	N. Does not approve of her husband's involvement with the Klan
A	15. SUTTER	O. Sara's dog that is killed by the Klan
C	16. PETTIBONE	P. Saw the person who shot Ira Hirsh
G	17. LEWIS	Q. Leanora helps him and they become friends.
O	18. JERRY	R. Is a bootlegger on the side to earn extra money
F	19. HIRSH	S. Shot Ira Hirsh
M	20. LEANORA	T. Tries to rescue his girlfriend from the orphanage

II. MULTIPLE CHOICE

D 1. How do Harvey and Viola Pettibone feel about the Ku Klux Klan?
- A. They both want to join.
- B. Viola wants to join and Harvey doesn't.
- C. They are both against joining.
- D. Harvey wants to join and Viola doesn't.

A 2. What is Leanora's relationship with Mr. Field?
- A. She becomes friends with him and enjoys listening to him talk.
- B. She starts to look at him as more of a father than her real dad.
- C. She gets bored with all his rambling and wishes he would hurry and get better.
- D. She begins to hate him since he obviously doesn't like black people.

D 3. What happens to Ira Hirsh?
- A. He is severely beaten.
- B. He is hanged.
- C. He is tarred and feathered.
- D. He is shot.

B 4. Why does Merlin Van Tornhout run away?
- A. He is tired of being a part of the Klan and wants out. He knows he wouldn't be able to just quit, so he runs away.
- B. He can't follow through with what the Klan wants him to do, so Harvey tells him to leave town before the Klan comes after him.
- C. His father is beating him, and he can't take it anymore.
- D. He runs away to be with his girlfriend, Mary. The two work out a plan to get married without anyone knowing.

C 5. What does the KKK do to keep up the appearance that they are serving the community?

A. They help the church raise money for the poor.

B. All the members attend church regularly.

C. They deliver baskets the needy and give money to the poor.

D. They buy clothes and school supplies for kids who come from poor families.

A 6. Why does Esther stand on the railroad tracks and refuse to move as a train approaches?

A. She was told her mother took a train to heaven. She thinks that all people who die get to heaven by train, and she wants to stop the train so she can get on and take her mother some flowers in heaven.

B. She misses her friends and family in New York but doesn't have enough money to visit them. She stands on the tracks hoping the train conductor will feel bad for her and let her go to New York for free.

C. She finds a litter of baby kittens on the train tracks and is trying to save them. As the train approaches, she stands in the way to stop it before it hits the kittens.

D. She enjoys the circus animals so much she wants to see them one last time before they leave town. The animals have been loaded on the train, and she tries to stop it.

A 7. What happens to Merlin Van Tornhout when he picks up a fellow Klansman on the way to a KKK meeting?

A. The man pulls out a knife and steals Merlin's car.

B. The man agrees to help Merlin get his girlfriend out of the orphanage.

C. The man tells Merlin he will help get him promoted to a higher positon in the KKK.

D. The man beats up Merlin and steals his wallet.

B 8. Mr. Field offers Leanora gifts that she would love to have. Each time he offers her something she wants, she declines his offer. Why doesn't she take his gifts when she wants them so much?

A. By taking the gifts she would feel obligated to continue working for him at a time when she is hoping to stop soon.

B. She is worried people will think she is stealing the items from him.

C. Her father won't let her take handouts from others. He thinks they are doing just fine on their own.

D. She thinks it is improper for a black girl to take gifts from a white man.

C 9. What groups does the KKK target?

A. Protestants, black people, and poor people
B. Catholics, poor people, and black people
C. Catholics, black people, and Jewish people
D. Protestants, black people, and foreigners

A 10. Who saw the person who shot Ira Hirsh?

A. Esther Hirsh
B. Iris Weaver
C. Harvey Pettibone
D. Leanora Sutter

IV. VOCABULARY

Answer	No.	Word	Letter	Definition
M	1.	INCITING	A.	Misleading; to make others believe something that is not true
I	2.	INORDINATE	B.	Tame; gentle; kind
G	3.	ENDURE	C.	Firm; strong; having endurance
O	4.	FIERCE	D.	Punishment or harassment usually of a severe nature on the basis of race, religion, or political opinion
L	5.	WIELD	E.	Very impressive because of great size, stately appearance, or dignity
A	6.	DECEPTIVE	F.	Reprimand or criticize harshly and usually angrily
T	7.	VIGILANT	G.	Carry on despite hardships
N	8.	UNSCRUPULOUS	H.	Looked intently, searchingly, or with difficulty
R	9.	PINNACLE	I.	Exceeding reasonable limits; uncontrolled
F	10.	SCOLD	J.	Future state of the wicked; damnation; hell
S	11.	VEXED	K.	Conflict; struggle; clash
C	12.	STOUT	L.	Exercise power, or influence as in ruling or dominating
Q	13.	RATTLED	M.	Stirring up, encouraging or prompting into action
D	14.	PERSECUTION	N.	Without principles
P	15.	ENTWINED	O.	Furiously intense; wild; violent in force
H	16.	PEERED	P.	Around or twisted together
K	17.	STRIFE	Q.	Flustered; unnerved; confused
B	18.	MEEK	R.	The highest point, as with success, power, or fame
E	19.	IMPOSING	S.	Irritated; annoyed
J	20.	PERDITION	T.	On the alert; watchful

Witness MULTIPLE CHOICE UNIT TEST 2

I. MATCHING/IDENTIFY

____ 1.	LEOPOLD	A.	Was kicked out of the KKK
____ 2.	IRA	B.	Klan thinks this family is worse than the Sutters.
____ 3.	IRIS	C.	Shot Ira Hirsh
____ 4.	REYNARD	D.	She is like a mother to Esther.
____ 5.	ESTHER	E.	He gives Merlin the keys to his business.
____ 6.	JOHNNY	F.	____ begins to have doubts about the Klan when they get more violent.
____ 7.	MARY	G.	Sara's dog that is killed by the Klan
____ 8.	PERCELLE	H.	Person in charge of maintaining peace in the town
____ 9.	SARA	I.	Leanora helps him and they become friends.
____ 10.	FITZGERALD	J.	Hassles Leanora about her race
____ 11.	HARVEY	K.	Wants to be married in KKK robes
____ 12.	FIELD	L.	Clears Merlin's name
____ 13.	SUTTER	M.	Rich, white boy who was murdered
____ 14.	PETTIBONE	N.	Saw the person who shot Ira Hirsh
____ 15.	LEWIS	O.	Owns a shoe store in town
____ 16.	FRANKS	P.	______ and Loeb kill a teenage boy in Chicago.
____ 17.	JERRY	Q.	She was stuck in a wagon in the cold for too long and later died: Mrs. ______.
____ 18.	REEVES	R.	Was suffocated by a sandbank cave-in
____ 19.	HIRSH	S.	Is a bootlegger on the side to earn extra money
____ 20.	LEANORA	T.	Helps save Ira Hirsh

II. MULTIPLE CHOICE

1. Why does Ira Hirsh consider moving out of Sara Chickering's house?
   A. Business is slow at the shoe store since many people in the Klan are boycotting his store. He can no longer afford to pay Sara a fair amount and wants to leave to allow her to rent his room to someone who can pay her.
   B. Someone throws a rock through Sara's window with a note attached. He wants to move out of the house so that the KKK will leave Sara alone.
   C. Sara has been comparing him to other men she has known in the past. He is worried she is starting to have feelings for him and wants to leave to avoid hurting her.
   D. Esther is getting too attached to Sara. He is worried that his daughter will keep bothering her and wants to leave before they wear out their welcome.

2. What is Leanora's relationship with Mr. Field?
   A. She becomes friends with him and enjoys listening to him talk.
   B. She begins to hate him since he obviously doesn't like black people.
   C. She starts to look at him as more of a father than her real dad.
   D. She gets bored with all his rambling and wishes he would hurry and get better.

3. Why does Johnny Reeves get kicked out of the KKK?
   A. He backs out of helping kill Mr. Sutter. His disobedience gets him kicked out.
   B. A "loose" woman shows up claiming that Johnny is the father of her baby. He gets kicked out for being an immoral man.
   C. His mother writes a letter saying she caught him in an inappropriate situation with a young school girl. He gets kicked out because they won't tolerate that type of behavior.
   D. They are tired of him being too controlling and dominant. He is kicked out so someone else can take power.

4. What happens to Ira Hirsh?
   A. He is shot.
   B. He is severely beaten.
   C. He is hanged.
   D. He is tarred and feathered.

5. What does the KKK want Merlin Van Tornhout to do?
   A. Put poison in the Sutters' well
   B. Kidnap Esther
   C. Beat up Leanora
   D. Burn down Mr. Hirsh's shoe store

6. Why does Merlin Van Tornhout run away?
   A. His father is beating him, and he can't take it anymore.
   B. He runs away to be with his girlfriend, Mary. The two work out a plan to get married without anyone knowing.
   C. He is tired of being a part of the Klan and wants out. He knows he wouldn't be able to just quit, so he runs away.
   D. He can't follow through with what the Klan wants him to do, so Harvey tells him to leave town before the Klan comes after him.

7. Why does Esther stand on the railroad tracks and refuse to move as a train approaches?
   A. She was told her mother took a train to heaven. She thinks that all people who die get to heaven by train, and she wants to stop the train so she can get on and take her mother some flowers in heaven.
   B. She finds a litter of baby kittens on the train tracks and is trying to save them. As the train approaches, she stands in the way to stop it before it hits the kittens.
   C. She enjoys the circus animals so much she wants to see them one last time before they leave town. The animals have been loaded on the train, and she tries to stop it.
   D. She misses her friends and family in New York but doesn't have enough money to visit them. She stands on the tracks hoping the train conductor will feel bad for her and let her go to New York for free.

8. What could Merlin Van Tornhout do to advance in the KKK?
   A. Help them steal more wood to make crosses
   B. Vandalize Ira Hirsh's shoe shop
   C. Give them the keys to the newspaper office
   D. Kill Leanora's father

9. What groups does the KKK target?
   A. Catholics, poor people, and black people
   B. Protestants, black people, and foreigners
   C. Catholics, black people, and Jewish people
   D. Protestants, black people, and poor people

10. Who clears Merlin's name and provides evidence that he did not shoot Ira Hirsh?

A. Mr. Sutter

B. Esther Hirsh

C. Leanora Sutter

D. Sara Chickering

III. ESSAY

1. How does each character grow over the course of the novel?

2. Why did the author choose to write a story from 11 different points of view? How did this affect the novel and its themes?

IV. VOCABULARY

____ 1.	INCITING	A.	Punishment or harassment usually of a severe nature on the basis of race, religion, or political opinion
____ 2.	LYNCHED	B.	Belonging to neither side in a controversy
____ 3.	NEUTRAL	C.	Formal request
____ 4.	ENDURE	D.	Lacking food, clothing, and shelter
____ 5.	RUBBISH	E.	Very impressive because of great size, stately appearance, or dignity
____ 6.	WIELD	F.	Exercise power, or influence as in ruling or dominating
____ 7.	DECEPTIVE	G.	Nonsense; worthless material; garbage
____ 8.	DESTITUTE	H.	Without principles
____ 9.	UNSCRUPULOUS	I.	Extracting or expelling by twisting or compression
____ 10.	PINNACLE	J.	Carry on despite hardships
____ 11.	VEXED	K.	Awkwardly tall or long-limbed
____ 12.	DICTATES	L.	Irritated; annoyed
____ 13.	GANGLING	M.	Misleading; to make others believe something that is not true
____ 14.	PERSECUTION	N.	Guiding principles
____ 15.	WRINGING	O.	Tame; gentle; kind
____ 16.	STRIFE	P.	The highest point, as with success, power, or fame
____ 17.	PETITION	Q.	Hanged, as by a mob, without due process of the law
____ 18.	MEEK	R.	Future state of the wicked; damnation; hell
____ 19.	IMPOSING	S.	Stirring up, encouraging or prompting into action
____ 20.	PERDITION	T.	Conflict; struggle; clash

Witness MULTIPLE CHOICE UNIT TEST 2 Answer Key

I. MATCHING/IDENTIFY

P	1. LEOPOLD	A. Was kicked out of the KKK
O	2. IRA	B. Klan thinks this family is worse than the Sutters.
S	3. IRIS	C. Shot Ira Hirsh
E	4. REYNARD	D. She is like a mother to Esther.
N	5. ESTHER	E. He gives Merlin the keys to his business.
C	6. JOHNNY	F. ____ begins to have doubts about the Klan when they get more violent.
K	7. MARY	G. Sara's dog that is killed by the Klan
H	8. PERCELLE	H. Person in charge of maintaining peace in the town
D	9. SARA	I. Leanora helps him and they become friends.
T	10. FITZGERALD	J. Hassles Leanora about her race
F	11. HARVEY	K. Wants to be married in KKK robes
I	12. FIELD	L. Clears Merlin's name
Q	13. SUTTER	M. Rich, white boy who was murdered
J	14. PETTIBONE	N. Saw the person who shot Ira Hirsh
R	15. LEWIS	O. Owns a shoe store in town
M	16. FRANKS	P. ______ and Loeb kill a teenage boy in Chicago.
G	17. JERRY	Q. She was stuck in a wagon in the cold for too long and later died: Mrs. _____.
A	18. REEVES	R. Was suffocated by a sandbank cave-in
B	19. HIRSH	S. Is a bootlegger on the side to earn extra money
L	20. LEANORA	T. Helps save Ira Hirsh

II. MULTIPLE CHOICE

B 1. Why does Ira Hirsh consider moving out of Sara Chickering's house?

A. Business is slow at the shoe store since many people in the Klan are boycotting his store. He can no longer afford to pay Sara a fair amount and wants to leave to allow her to rent his room to someone who can pay her.

B. Someone throws a rock through Sara's window with a note attached. He wants to move out of the house so that the KKK will leave Sara alone.

C. Sara has been comparing him to other men she has known in the past. He is worried she is starting to have feelings for him and wants to leave to avoid hurting her.

D. Esther is getting too attached to Sara. He is worried that his daughter will keep bothering her and wants to leave before they wear out their welcome.

A 2. What is Leanora's relationship with Mr. Field?

A. She becomes friends with him and enjoys listening to him talk.

B. She begins to hate him since he obviously doesn't like black people.

C. She starts to look at him as more of a father than her real dad.

D. She gets bored with all his rambling and wishes he would hurry and get better.

C 3. Why does Johnny Reeves get kicked out of the KKK?

A. He backs out of helping kill Mr. Sutter. His disobedience gets him kicked out.

B. A "loose" woman shows up claiming that Johnny is the father of her baby. He gets kicked out for being an immoral man.

C. His mother writes a letter saying she caught him in an inappropriate situation with a young school girl. He gets kicked out because they won't tolerate that type of behavior.

D. They are tired of him being too controlling and dominant. He is kicked out so someone else can take power.

A 4. What happens to Ira Hirsh?

A. He is shot.

B. He is severely beaten.

C. He is hanged.

D. He is tarred and feathered.

A 5. What does the KKK want Merlin Van Tornhout to do?

A. Put poison in the Sutters' well

B. Kidnap Esther

C. Beat up Leanora

D. Burn down Mr. Hirsh's shoe store

D 6. Why does Merlin Van Tornhout run away?

A. His father is beating him, and he can't take it anymore.

B. He runs away to be with his girlfriend, Mary. The two work out a plan to get married without anyone knowing.

C. He is tired of being a part of the Klan and wants out. He knows he wouldn't be able to just quit, so he runs away.

D. He can't follow through with what the Klan wants him to do, so Harvey tells him to leave town before the Klan comes after him.

A 7. Why does Esther stand on the railroad tracks and refuse to move as a train approaches?

A. She was told her mother took a train to heaven. She thinks that all people who die get to heaven by train, and she wants to stop the train so she can get on and take her mother some flowers in heaven.

B. She finds a litter of baby kittens on the train tracks and is trying to save them. As the train approaches, she stands in the way to stop it before it hits the kittens.

C. She enjoys the circus animals so much she wants to see them one last time before they leave town. The animals have been loaded on the train, and she tries to stop it.

D. She misses her friends and family in New York but doesn't have enough money to visit them. She stands on the tracks hoping the train conductor will feel bad for her and let her go to New York for free.

C 8. What could Merlin Van Tornhout do to advance in the KKK?

A. Help them steal more wood to make crosses

B. Vandalize Ira Hirsh's shoe shop

C. Give them the keys to the newspaper office

D. Kill Leanora's father

C 9. What groups does the KKK target?

A. Catholics, poor people, and black people

B. Protestants, black people, and foreigners

C. Catholics, black people, and Jewish people

D. Protestants, black people, and poor people

C 10. Who clears Merlin's name and provides evidence that he did not shoot Ira Hirsh?

A. Mr. Sutter

B. Esther Hirsh

C. Leanora Sutter

D. Sara Chickering

IV. VOCABULARY

S	1. INCITING	A. Punishment or harassment usually of a severe nature on the basis of race, religion, or political opinion
Q	2. LYNCHED	B. Belonging to neither side in a controversy
B	3. NEUTRAL	C. Formal request
J	4. ENDURE	D. Lacking food, clothing, and shelter
G	5. RUBBISH	E. Very impressive because of great size, stately appearance, or dignity
F	6. WIELD	F. Exercise power, or influence as in ruling or dominating
M	7. DECEPTIVE	G. Nonsense; worthless material; garbage
D	8. DESTITUTE	H. Without principles
H	9. UNSCRUPULOUS	I. Extracting or expelling by twisting or compression
P	10. PINNACLE	J. Carry on despite hardships
L	11. VEXED	K. Awkwardly tall or long-limbed
N	12. DICTATES	L. Irritated; annoyed
K	13. GANGLING	M. Misleading; to make others believe something that is not true
A	14. PERSECUTION	N. Guiding principles
I	15. WRINGING	O. Tame; gentle; kind
T	16. STRIFE	P. The highest point, as with success, power, or fame
C	17. PETITION	Q. Hanged, as by a mob, without due process of the law
O	18. MEEK	R. Future state of the wicked; damnation; hell
E	19. IMPOSING	S. Stirring up, encouraging or prompting into action
R	20. PERDITION	T. Conflict; struggle; clash

UNIT RESOURCE MATERIALS

BULLETIN BOARD IDEAS *Witness*

1. Save one corner of the board for the best of students' *Witness* writing assignments.
2. Take one of the word search puzzles from the extra activities packet and with a marker copy it over in a large size on the bulletin board. Write the clue words to find to one side. Invite students prior to and after class to find the words and circle them on the bulletin board.
3. Write several of the most significant quotations from the book onto the board on brightly colored paper.
4. Make a bulletin board listing the vocabulary words for this unit. As you complete sections of the novel and discuss the vocabulary for each section, write the definitions on the bulletin board. (If your board is one students face frequently, it will help them learn the words.)
5. Post photos and information about people who have been victims of a hate crime. Many teenage magazines run feature stories on teenagers who have been victims of teen hate crimes and students would most likely enjoy articles from magazines they like to read.
6. Create a bulletin board with a tolerance theme. Place facts, information, and tips for practicing tolerance on the board. You may also want to have information about organizations who are fighting hate crimes with contact information and websites to get involved.
7. Make a bulletin board with colorful copies of other books Karen Hesse has written. Write a short tease for the books to get students interested.
8. Decorate your bulletin board with information about the time period. Put examples of clothing, art, music, etc on the bulletin board to help students learn about the 1920's.
9. Make a bulletin board advertising other young adult historical fiction novels. Print out colorful copies of the covers of these other historical fiction novels and attach a short summary or excerpt.
10. Create a KWL chart for the unit on the bulletin board with your students.

MORE ACTIVITIES *Witness*

1. Have students design a new book cover (front and back and inside flaps) for *Witness.*
2. Have students design a bulletin board (ready to be put up; not just sketched) for *Witness.*
3. Have students choose one portion of the book (with sufficient action) to rewrite with dialogue. In conjunction with this assignment, have students write a composition explaining the difficulties they encountered in changing from one written form to another.
4. Have students write out the characters in the book and cast famous actors and actresses for an updated movie version of the novel. Instruct students to write a brief explanation as to why the actor/actress they selected would be perfect for the part.
5. Have students create a soundtrack for *Witness*. Have students burn a cd of the songs, design a cd cover, and include a brief explanation as to why they selected each song.
6. Have students further explore the time period. Instruct students to use the internet to find more information about life in the 1920's.
7. Have students research the historical figures Karen Hesse mentions in her novel. Ask students to create a short biography about each one.
8. Have students research the civil rights movement. Ask students to create a poster to display in the classroom to teach others more about the movement.
9. Have students research the women's rights movement. Ask students to create a poster to display in the classroom to teach others more about the movement.
10. Have students devise a plan to promote tolerance in their community.
11. Have students write a continuation to the story. Ask them to write about the lives of characters five years after the end of the story.
12. Have students watch the video associated with the Laramie Project and write a short summary about what they learned.
13. Have students create a timeline for the actions and events in each individual character's life.
14. Have students find a poem on hatred. Have them also find a poem on tolerance. Ask them to complete a Venn Diagram on the two poems.
15. Have students find commercials and advertisements from the time period and compare them with commercials and advertisements now.
16. Have students read the book Leanora mentions by Helen Keller, *The World I Live In.*
17. Have students do further research on genocide and other large scale hate crimes nationally and internationally.
18. Have students select a character from the book and complete the "I Am" poem from that character's point of view.

19. Provide each student with a sheet of construction paper, magazines, scissors, and glue. Ask students to think about what it means to be an American. Next, have them find words and images in the magazines that portray what it means to be American. Prompt students to think of the different types of people in society and the various ways in which they contribute to this country. Students may also add their own words and hand-drawn pictures in this collage.

    When students have completed their collage, bring the class back together to discuss the images and words used to describe Americans. Try to lead the discussion to how different cultures contribute to America and use this time to introduce the idea that America is often referred to as a great melting pot. Talk about how each culture in our country has contributed to who our country is today, and ask students to brainstorm ways in which our country is better due to the variety of people living in it. After this discussion, have students write a short response on the back of their collage about how they feel our country is better with the mixture of people living here.

    After students have turned in their collages, take pieces of yarn and put the collages together to assemble a quilt. You may want to have a couple students who finish assignments quickly work on this project over the next few days. In the center of the quilt, it might be a good idea to make a piece that allows viewers to know the topic of your quilt. After you have put the collages of your students together to form this quilt, hang it in your classroom for others to enjoy.

"I Am" Poem

Complete this "I am" poem. You may select any character from the book to do this poem about. Be sure to write from his or her point of view and think about the things he or she would feel. You may use some short one word answers, but do not make each line only a few words. You should try to provide support from the novel to really develop this poem so that it reveals information and insight about the character you select.

I am (2 characteristics your character has)
I wonder (something your character wonders)
I hear (something real or imaginary your character hears)
I see (something real or imaginary your character sees)
I want (something your character desires)
I am (the first line of the poem repeated)

I pretend (something your character pretends to do)
I feel (something real or imaginary your character feels emotionally)
I touch (something real or imaginary your character would touch physically)
I worry (something your character worries about)
I cry (something that makes your character upset)
I am (the first line of the poem repeated)

I understand (something your character knows)
I say (something your character believes in)
I dream (something your character would dream about)
I try (something your character makes an effort to do)
I hope (something your character hopes for)
I am (the first line of the poem repeated)

UNIT WORD LIST *Witness*

No.	Word	Clue/Definition
1.	BABY	Percelle found one wrapped in a newspaper.
2.	BRANDED	The KKK did this to Johnny with the letters KKK.
3.	BRIDGE	Johnny Reeves jumps off a ___________ because he is afraid of the Klan.
4.	BROOMS	Sale items that caused a stampede
5.	CANE	Mr. Fields' weapon at the courhouse
6.	CAR	Klansmen stole this from Merlin.
7.	COLLEGE	Iris paid for her siblings to go there.
8.	CROSS	The KKK burns one on July 4th.
9.	ESTHER	Saw the person who shot Ira Hirsh
10.	FEAR	Merlin runs away because he feels this.
11.	FIELD	Leanora helps him and they become friends.
12.	FITZGERALD	Helps save Ira Hirsh
13.	FRANKS	Rich, white boy who was murdered
14.	GALOSHES	Mary struts around in these.
15.	HARVEY	____ begins to have doubts about the Klan when they get more violent.
16.	HATE	Characteristic of Klan members
17.	HEAVEN	Esther thinks her mother took a train to this place.
18.	HIRSH	Klan thinks this family is worse than the Sutters.
19.	HOLLOWEEN	Holiday Esther enjoys celebrating
20.	HOME	Johnny says women are happiest at this place.
21.	HOTEL	Place where Harvey and Klan do damage
22.	IRA	Owns a shoe store in town
23.	IRIS	Is a bootlegger on the side to earn extra money
24.	JERRY	Sara's dog that is killed by the Klan
25.	JEWS	Group the Klan targets
26.	JOHNNY	Shot Ira Hirsh
27.	KELLER	Leanora gets a signed book from her.
28.	KIDNAPPING	Merlin is charged with this.
29.	KKK	Group that harasses people in the town
30.	LEANORA	Clears Merlin's name
31.	LEOPOLD	______ and Loeb kill a teenage boy in Chicago.
32.	LEWIS	Was suffocated by a sandbank cave-in
33.	MARRIED	Sara never did this.
34.	MARY	Wants to be married in KKK robes
35.	MERLIN	Tries to rescue his girlfriend from the orphanage
36.	MURDER	Leopold and Loeb are charged with this.
37.	NEWSPAPER	Where the town learns how Leanora rescued Esther

No.	Word	Clue/Definition
38.	PERCELLE	Person in charge of maintaining peace in the town
39.	PETTIBONE	Hassles Leanora about her race
40.	POISON	Merlin was supposed to put this in the Sutters' well.
41.	POOR	The Klan gives money to them.
42.	PRESIDENT	Coolidge was elected as this.
43.	REEVES	Was kicked out of the KKK
44.	REYNARD	He gives Merlin the keys to his business.
45.	ROCK	Someone threw this through Sara's window.
46.	SARA	She is like a mother to Esther.
47.	SCHOOL	Place where Leanora is most often teased about being black
48.	SUTTER	She was stuck in a wagon in the cold for too long and later died: Mrs. _____.
49.	TRAIN	Esther is almost hit by one of these
50.	VIOLA	Does not approve of her husband's involvement with the Klan
51.	VOTE	What women got the right to do; Iris Weaver was excited to do this
52.	WAGON	No one would help Leanora's family when they had a problem with this.

WORD SEACRCH Witness

P	E	T	T	I	B	O	N	E	V	I	O	L	A	C	F	F	C	Z	W
F	Z	F	I	T	Z	G	E	R	A	L	D	Z	S	Y	N	I	K	Z	C
D	K	L	K	I	D	N	A	P	P	I	N	G	Y	C	P	M	E	R	D
X	K	E	C	G	C	W	T	B	R	G	J	S	Q	P	H	B	Q	L	H
G	X	A	H	J	Z	D	N	R	M	J	X	S	M	R	S	O	T	P	D
C	P	N	Q	W	E	X	K	O	V	E	H	K	J	E	B	P	O	Z	B
R	V	O	R	D	T	N	C	O	M	R	O	N	T	S	V	A	T	L	C
Y	L	R	N	F	A	B	O	M	E	R	M	A	K	I	H	G	B	X	P
A	R	A	S	L	H	I	R	S	H	Y	E	R	E	D	R	U	M	Y	K
Q	R	V	L	O	K	O	T	I	S	N	A	F	E	E	Z	L	R	R	H
B	T	Q	T	Q	O	H	L	N	D	E	T	I	H	N	T	A	C	J	P
V	Q	E	W	P	E	V	F	H	F	G	R	N	C	T	M	R	G	D	T
H	L	K	D	R	A	N	Y	E	R	R	E	N	A	C	I	R	A	N	W
P	H	E	G	T	E	P	C	T	A	V	L	C	H	J	N	R	E	N	C
Z	E	T	W	K	S	E	J	M	A	Z	L	R	C	E	J	E	I	N	P
P	J	R	D	I	K	M	V	E	M	D	E	O	W	C	W	H	L	S	T
S	O	A	C	W	S	K	H	E	W	V	K	S	R	O	A	R	E	V	H
U	H	I	F	E	F	Y	R	X	S	S	P	S	L	R	G	R	O	O	G
T	N	N	S	B	L	L	N	T	T	A	F	L	V	P	O	N	P	T	X
T	N	T	Z	O	I	L	P	H	P	D	O	E	T	C	N	G	O	E	J
E	Y	D	M	N	N	P	E	E	L	H	Y	K	E	G	E	L	L	O	C
R	Q	S	S	W	Z	C	R	G	A	L	O	S	H	E	S	F	D	B	C

BABY	FITZGERALD	IRIS	MARY	ROCK
BRANDED	FRANKS	JERRY	MERLIN	SARA
BRIDGE	GALOSHES	JEWS	MURDER	SCHOOL
BROOMS	HARVEY	JOHNNY	NEWSPAPER	SUTTER
CANE	HATE	KELLER	PERCELLE	TRAIN
CAR	HEAVEN	KIDNAPPING	PETTIBONE	VIOLA
COLLEGE	HIRSH	KKK	POISON	VOTE
CROSS	HOLLOWEEN	LEANORA	POOR	WAGON
ESTHER	HOME	LEOPOLD	PRESIDENT	
FEAR	HOTEL	LEWIS	REEVES	
FIELD	IRA	MARRIED	REYNARD	

WORD SEACRCH ANSWER KEY Witness

P	E	T	T	I	B	O	N	E	V	I	O	L	A		F				
		F	I	T	Z	G	E	R	A	L	D		S			I			
		L	K	I	D	N	A	P	P	I	N	G		C			E		
		E						B						P	H			L	
		A				D		R		J		S		R		O			D
		N			E		K	O		E	H	K		E	B		O		
		O		D	T		C	O		R	O	N		S		A		L	
		R	N		A	B	O	M	E	R	M	A		I			B		
A	R	A	S		H	I	R	S	H	Y	E	R	E	D	R	U	M	Y	
	R			O		O	T	I			A	F	E	E			R		
B			T		O	H			D	E		I		N		A			
		E		P	E				F	G	R	N		T	M				
	L		D	R	A	N	Y	E	R	R	E	N	A	C	I	R	A	N	
P		E			E				A	V	L	C			N	R	E		
	E	T	W	K		E	J	M	A		L	R		E		E	I		
P	J	R		I	K		V	E	M		E	O	W	C	W	H	L	S	
S	O	A	C		S	K	H	E	W		K	S		O	A		E	V	
U	H	I		E			R		S	S	P	S	L	R	G	R	O	O	
T	N	N	S		L	L				A		L	V		O		P	T	
T	N			O	I	L			P		O	E			N		O	E	
E	Y			N	N		E	E		H	Y		E	G	E	L	L	O	C
R							R	G	A	L	O	S	H	E	S		D		

BABY	FITZGERALD	IRIS	MARY	ROCK
BRANDED	FRANKS	JERRY	MERLIN	SARA
BRIDGE	GALOSHES	JEWS	MURDER	SCHOOL
BROOMS	HARVEY	JOHNNY	NEWSPAPER	SUTTER
CANE	HATE	KELLER	PERCELLE	TRAIN
CAR	HEAVEN	KIDNAPPING	PETTIBONE	VIOLA
COLLEGE	HIRSH	KKK	POISON	VOTE
CROSS	HOLLOWEEN	LEANORA	POOR	WAGON
ESTHER	HOME	LEOPOLD	PRESIDENT	
FEAR	HOTEL	LEWIS	REEVES	
FIELD	IRA	MARRIED	REYNARD	

CROSSWORD Witness

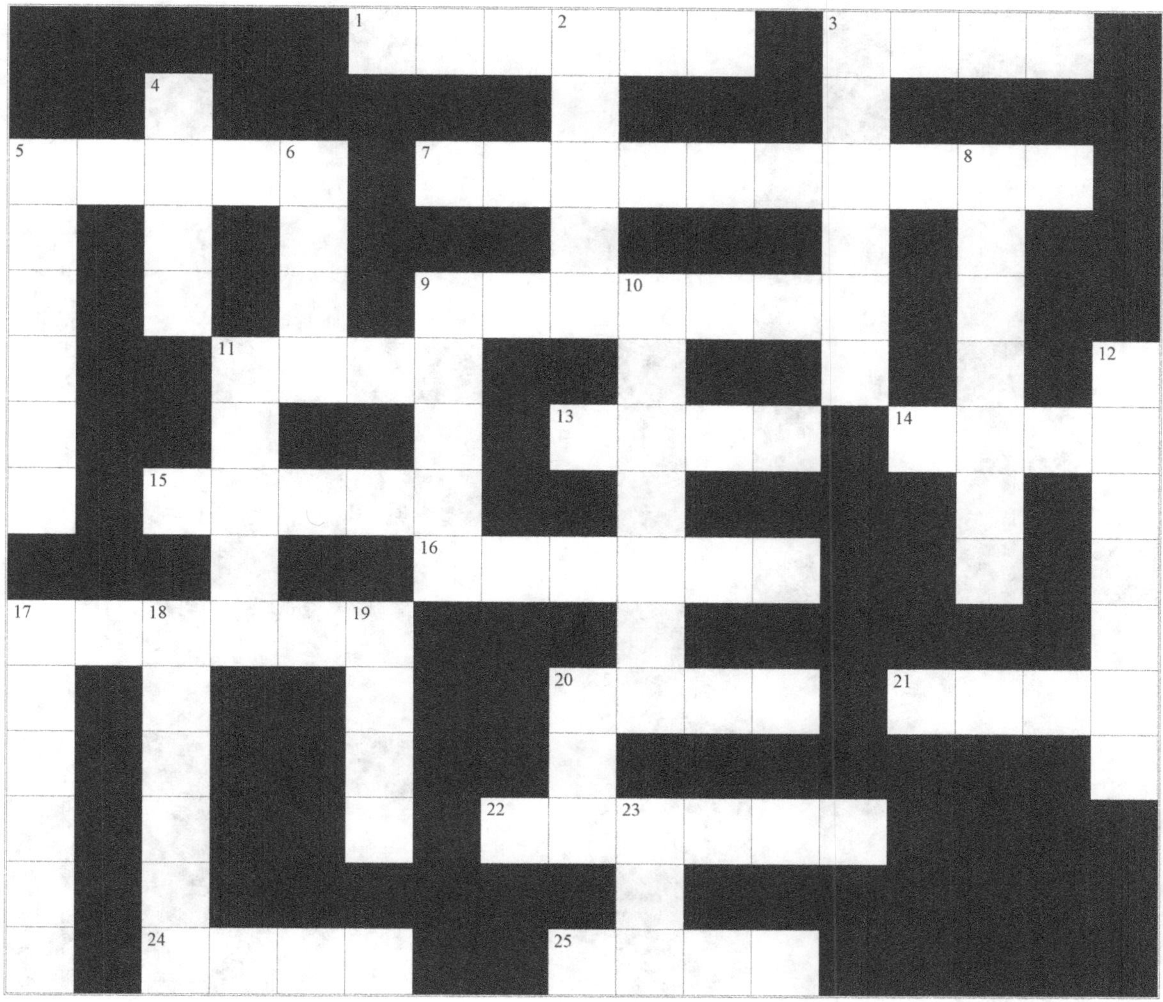

Across
1. Saw the person who shot Ira Hirsh
3. Characteristic of Klan members
5. Klan thinks this family is worse than the Sutters'.
7. Helps save Ira Hirsh
9. Iris paid for her siblings to go there.
11. Merlin runs away because he feels this.
13. Wants to be married in KKK robes
14. The Klan give money to them.
15. Was suffocated by a sandbank cave-in
16. Place where Leanora is most often teased about being black
17. Leopold and Loeb are charged with this.
20. Mr. Fields' weapon at the courhouse
21. What women got the right to do; Iris Weaver was excited to do this
22. Johnny Reeves jumps off a ___________ because he is afraid of the Klan.
24. She is like a mother to Esther.
25. Percelle found this wrapped in a newspaper.

Down
2. Place where Harvey and Klan do damage
3. ____ begins to have doubts about the Klan when they get more violent.
4. Is a bootlegger on the side to earn extra money
5. Esther thinks her mother took a train to this place.
6. Johnny says women are happiest at this place.
8. __________ and Loeb kill a teenage boy in Chicago and face the death penalty.
9. One of the first acts the KKK does; __________ burning on July 4th
10. Clears Merlin's name
11. Leanora helps him and they become friends.
12. The KKK did this to Johnny with the letters KKK.
17. Tries to rescue his girlfriend from the orphanage
18. Was kicked out of the KKK
19. Someone threw this through Sara's window.
20. Klansmen stole this from Merlin.
23. Owns a shoe store in town

CROSSWORD ANSWER KEY Witness

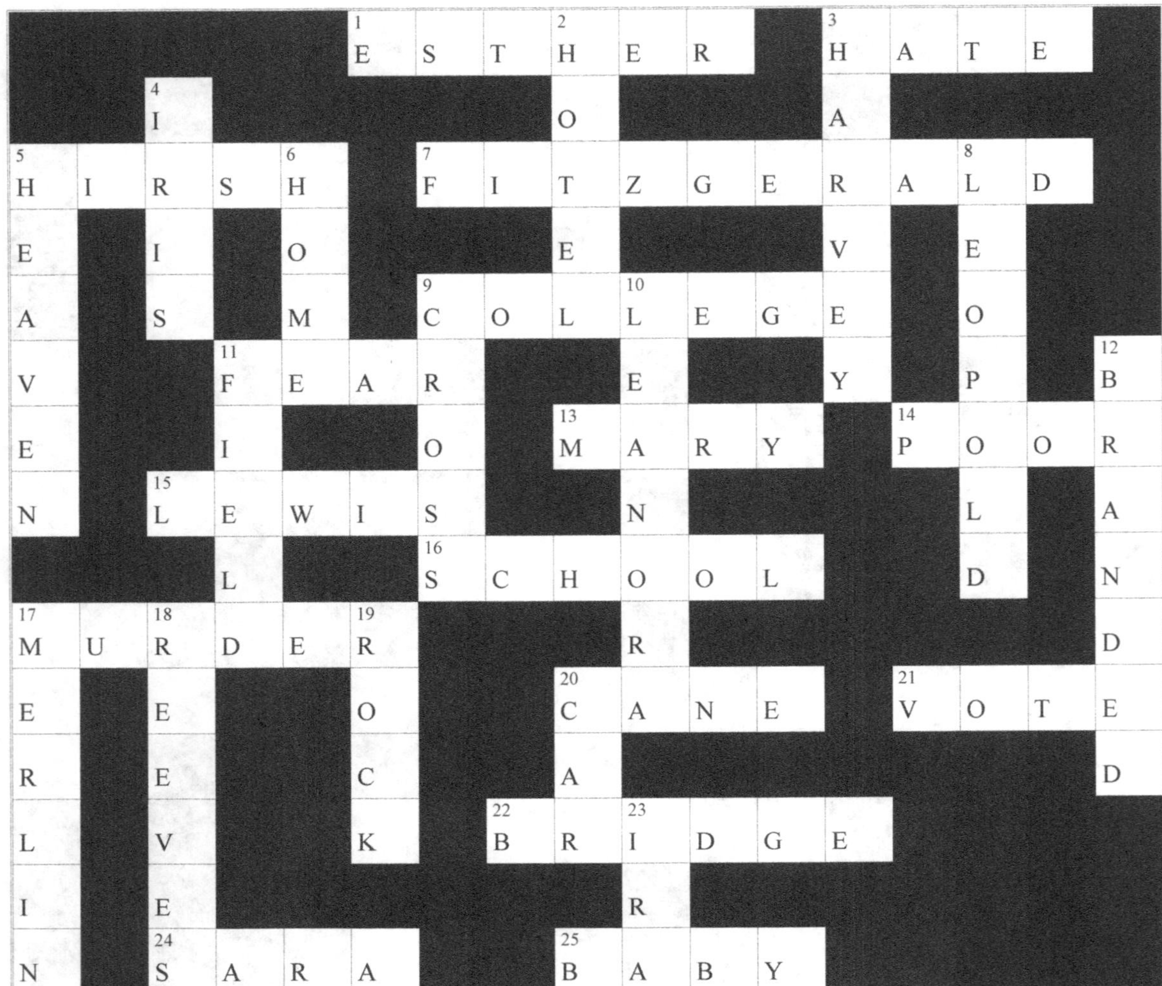

Across
1. Saw the person who shot Ira Hirsh
3. Characteristic of Klan members
5. Klan thinks this family is worse than the Sutters'.
7. Helps save Ira Hirsh
9. Iris paid for her siblings to go there.
11. Merlin runs away because he feels this.
13. Wants to be married in KKK robes
14. The Klan give money to them.
15. Was suffocated by a sandbank cave-in
16. Place where Leanora is most often teased about being black
17. Leopold and Loeb are charged with this.
20. Mr. Fields' weapon at the courhouse
21. What women got the right to do; Iris Weaver was excited to do this
22. Johnny Reeves jumps off a ___________ because he is afraid of the Klan.
24. She is like a mother to Esther.
25. Percelle found this wrapped in a newspaper.

Down
2. Place where Harvey and Klan do damage
3. ____ begins to have doubts about the Klan when they get more violent.
4. Is a bootlegger on the side to earn extra money
5. Esther thinks her mother took a train to this place.
6. Johnny says women are happiest at this place.
8. __________ and Loeb kill a teenage boy in Chicago and face the death penalty.
9. One of the first acts the KKK does; __________ burning on July 4th
10. Clears Merlin's name
11. Leanora helps him and they become friends.
12. The KKK did this to Johnny with the letters KKK.
17. Tries to rescue his girlfriend from the orphanage
18. Was kicked out of the KKK
19. Someone threw this through Sara's window.
20. Klansmen stole this from Merlin.
23. Owns a shoe store in town

MATCHING 1 *Witness*

____ 1.	LEANORA	A.	Tries to rescue his girlfriend from the orphanage
____ 2.	PERCELLE	B.	Leanora helps him and they become friends.
____ 3.	JOHNNY	C.	Clears Merlin's name
____ 4.	ESTHER	D.	Characteristic of Klan members
____ 5.	LEWIS	E.	Is a bootlegger on the side to earn extra money
____ 6.	PETTIBONE	F.	He gives Merlin the keys to his business.
____ 7.	REYNARD	G.	Was suffocated by a sandbank cave-in
____ 8.	IRIS	H.	Helps save Ira Hirsh
____ 9.	MERLIN	I.	Shot Ira Hirsh
____ 10.	SARA	J.	Merlin is charged with this.
____ 11.	FITZGERALD	K.	______ and Loeb kill a teenage boy in Chicago.
____ 12.	FEAR	L.	Saw the person who shot Ira Hirsh
____ 13.	HATE	M.	Person in charge of maintaining peace in the town
____ 14.	MURDER	N.	Hassles Leanora about her race
____ 15.	KIDNAPPING	O.	Merlin runs away because he feels this.
____ 16.	HIRSH	P.	Was kicked out of the KKK
____ 17.	REEVES	Q.	Klan thinks this family is worse than the Sutters.
____ 18.	FIELD	R.	____ begins to have doubts about the Klan when they get more violent.
____ 19.	HARVEY	S.	She is like a mother to Esther.
____ 20.	LEOPOLD	T.	Leopold and Loeb are charged with this.

MATCHING 1 ANSWER KEY *Witness*

C	1. LEANORA	A. Tries to rescue his girlfriend from the orphanage
M	2. PERCELLE	B. Leanora helps him and they become friends.
I	3. JOHNNY	C. Clears Merlin's name
L	4. ESTHER	D. Characteristic of Klan members
G	5. LEWIS	E. Is a bootlegger on the side to earn extra money
N	6. PETTIBONE	F. He gives Merlin the keys to his business.
F	7. REYNARD	G. Was suffocated by a sandbank cave-in
E	8. IRIS	H. Helps save Ira Hirsh
A	9. MERLIN	I. Shot Ira Hirsh
S	10. SARA	J. Merlin is charged with this.
H	11. FITZGERALD	K. ______ and Loeb kill a teenage boy in Chicago.
O	12. FEAR	L. Saw the person who shot Ira Hirsh
D	13. HATE	M. Person in charge of maintaining peace in the town
T	14. MURDER	N. Hassles Leanora about her race
J	15. KIDNAPPING	O. Merlin runs away because he feels this.
Q	16. HIRSH	P. Was kicked out of the KKK
P	17. REEVES	Q. Klan thinks this family is worse than the Sutters.
B	18. FIELD	R. ____ begins to have doubts about the Klan when they get more violent.
R	19. HARVEY	S. She is like a mother to Esther.
K	20. LEOPOLD	T. Leopold and Loeb are charged with this.

MATCHING 2 *Witness*

____ 1.	LEANORA	A.	Does not approve of her husband's involvement with the Klan
____ 2.	JOHNNY	B.	Owns a shoe store in town
____ 3.	ESTHER	C.	Shot Ira Hirsh
____ 4.	PETTIBONE	D.	Tries to rescue his girlfriend from the orphanage
____ 5.	REYNARD	E.	Saw the person who shot Ira Hirsh
____ 6.	IRIS	F.	Leanora helps him and they become friends.
____ 7.	MERLIN	G.	Rich, white boy who was murdered
____ 8.	IRA	H.	He gives Merlin the keys to his business.
____ 9.	VIOLA	I.	Was kicked out of the KKK
____ 10.	MARY	J.	Is a bootlegger on the side to earn extra money
____ 11.	SARA	K.	She is like a mother to Esther.
____ 12.	KELLER	L.	Clears Merlin's name
____ 13.	COLLEGE	M.	Leanora gets a signed book from her.
____ 14.	REEVES	N.	Merlin was supposed to put this in the Sutters' well.
____ 15.	FRANKS	O.	____ begins to have doubts about the Klan when they get more violent.
____ 16.	SUTTER	P.	Wants to be married in KKK robes
____ 17.	FIELD	Q.	Helps save Ira Hirsh
____ 18.	HARVEY	R.	Iris paid for her siblings to go there.
____ 19.	FITZGERALD	S.	She was stuck in a wagon in the cold for too long and later died: Mrs. _____.
____ 20.	POISON	T.	Hassles Leanora about her race

MATCHING 2 ANSWER KEY *Witness*

L	1. LEANORA	A.	Does not approve of her husband's involvement with the Klan
C	2. JOHNNY	B.	Owns a shoe store in town
E	3. ESTHER	C.	Shot Ira Hirsh
T	4. PETTIBONE	D.	Tries to rescue his girlfriend from the orphanage
H	5. REYNARD	E.	Saw the person who shot Ira Hirsh
J	6. IRIS	F.	Leanora helps him and they become friends.
D	7. MERLIN	G.	Rich, white boy who was murdered
B	8. IRA	H.	He gives Merlin the keys to his business.
A	9. VIOLA	I.	Was kicked out of the KKK
P	10. MARY	J.	Is a bootlegger on the side to earn extra money
K	11. SARA	K.	She is like a mother to Esther.
M	12. KELLER	L.	Clears Merlin's name
R	13. COLLEGE	M.	Leanora gets a signed book from her.
I	14. REEVES	N.	Merlin was supposed to put this in the Sutters' well.
G	15. FRANKS	O.	____ begins to have doubts about the Klan when they get more violent.
S	16. SUTTER	P.	Wants to be married in KKK robes
F	17. FIELD	Q.	Helps save Ira Hirsh
O	18. HARVEY	R.	Iris paid for her siblings to go there.
Q	19. FITZGERALD	S.	She was stuck in a wagon in the cold for too long and later died: Mrs. _____.
N	20. POISON	T.	Hassles Leanora about her race

JUGGLE LETTER 1 *Witness*

__________ = 1. PPGAKIINND
Merlin is charged with this.

__________ = 2. SEJW
Group the Klan targets

__________ = 3. OPOR
The Klan gives money to them.

__________ = 4. DRMURE
Leopold and Loeb are charged with this.

__________ = 5. POEDLLO
______ and Loeb kill a teenage boy in Chicago.

__________ = 6. AIR
Owns a shoe store in town

__________ = 7. NYRRADE
He gives Merlin the keys to his business.

__________ = 8. TBOIEPNTE
Hassles Leanora about her race

__________ = 9. RTESHE
Saw the person who shot Ira Hirsh

__________ = 10. NJOHNY
Shot Ira Hirsh

__________ = 11. OSAEGHLS
Mary struts around in these.

__________ = 12. REECEPLL
Person in charge of maintaining peace in the town

__________ = 13. ADGLEFZTRI
Helps save Ira Hirsh

__________ = 14. RVHYEA
____ begins to have doubts about the Klan when they get more violent.

__________ = 15. NKRSAF
Rich, white boy who was murdered

__________ = 16. REEEVS
Was kicked out of the KKK

__________ = 17. SHRIH
Klan thinks this family is worse than the Sutters.

__________ = 18. NEORAAL
Clears Merlin's name

JUGGLE LETTER 1 ANSWER KEY *Witness*

KIDNAPPING	= 1.	PPGAKIINND Merlin is charged with this.
JEWS	= 2.	SEJW Group the Klan targets
POOR	= 3.	OPOR The Klan gives money to them.
MURDER	= 4.	DRMURE Leopold and Loeb are charged with this.
LEOPOLD	= 5.	POEDLLO ______ and Loeb kill a teenage boy in Chicago.
IRA	= 6.	AIR Owns a shoe store in town
REYNARD	= 7.	NYRRADE He gives Merlin the keys to his business.
PETTIBONE	= 8.	TBOIEPNTE Hassles Leanora about her race
ESTHER	= 9.	RTESHE Saw the person who shot Ira Hirsh
JOHNNY	= 10.	NJOHNY Shot Ira Hirsh
GALOSHES	= 11.	OSAEGHLS Mary struts around in these.
PERCELLE	= 12.	REECEPLL Person in charge of maintaining peace in the town
FITZGERALD	= 13.	ADGLEFZTRI Helps save Ira Hirsh
HARVEY	= 14.	RVHYEA ____ begins to have doubts about the Klan when they get more violent.
FRANKS	= 15.	NKRSAF Rich, white boy who was murdered
REEVES	= 16.	REEEVS Was kicked out of the KKK
HIRSH	= 17.	SHRIH Klan thinks this family is worse than the Sutters.
LEANORA	= 18.	NEORAAL Clears Merlin's name

JUGGLE LETTER 2 *Witness*

________ = 1. RVAHYE
____ begins to have doubts about the Klan when they get more violent.

________ = 2. ERAF
Merlin runs away because he feels this.

________ = 3. HETA
Characteristic of Klan members

________ = 4. IINGNDKPAP
Merlin is charged with this.

________ = 5. OSPNOI
Merlin was supposed to put this in the Sutters' well.

________ = 6. VAOIL
Does not approve of her husband's involvement with the Klan

________ = 7. LNMRIE
Tries to rescue his girlfriend from the orphanage

________ = 8. SIRI
Is a bootlegger on the side to earn extra money

________ = 9. AERNRYD
He gives Merlin the keys to his business.

________ = 10. REEWAPPNS
Where the town learns how Leanora rescued Esther

________ = 11. ESIWL
Was suffocated by a sandbank cave-in

________ = 12. CAR
Klansmen stole this from Merlin.

________ = 13. ESRTEH
Saw the person who shot Ira Hirsh

________ = 14. NJYHNO
Shot Ira Hirsh

________ = 15. LEEPLERC
Person in charge of maintaining peace in the town

________ = 16. AASR
She is like a mother to Esther.

________ = 17. AELGTIRDFZ
Helps save Ira Hirsh

________ = 18. OAAELRN
Clears Merlin's name

JUGGLE LETTER 2 ANSWER KEY *Witness*

HARVEY	= 1.	RVAHYE ____ begins to have doubts about the Klan when they get more violent.
FEAR	= 2.	ERAF Merlin runs away because he feels this.
HATE	= 3.	HETA Characteristic of Klan members
KIDNAPPING	= 4.	IINGNDKPAP Merlin is charged with this.
POISON	= 5.	OSPNOI Merlin was supposed to put this in the Sutters' well.
VIOLA	= 6.	VAOIL Does not approve of her husband's involvement with the Klan
MERLIN	= 7.	LNMRIE Tries to rescue his girlfriend from the orphanage
IRIS	= 8.	SIRI Is a bootlegger on the side to earn extra money
REYNARD	= 9.	AERNRYD He gives Merlin the keys to his business.
NEWSPAPER	= 10.	REEWAPPNS Where the town learns how Leanora rescued Esther
LEWIS	= 11.	ESIWL Was suffocated by a sandbank cave-in
CAR	= 12.	CAR Klansmen stole this from Merlin.
ESTHER	= 13.	ESRTEH Saw the person who shot Ira Hirsh
JOHNNY	= 14.	NJYHNO Shot Ira Hirsh
PERCELLE	= 15.	LEEPLERC Person in charge of maintaining peace in the town
SARA	= 16.	AASR She is like a mother to Esther.
FITZGERALD	= 17.	AELGTIRDFZ Helps save Ira Hirsh
LEANORA	= 18.	OAAELRN Clears Merlin's name

VOCABULARY RESOURCE MATERIALS

Witness Vocabulary

No.	Word	Clue/Definition
1.	ADVISING	Recommending; suggesting
2.	BRANDED	Symbol burned on with a hot iron
3.	BRIGADE	Large body of troops; a military unit
4.	CLERGYMAN	Christian minister
5.	CONDUCTED	The way a person acts, especially from the standpoint of morality and ethics
6.	CONSTABLE	Peace officer with less authority than a sheriff
7.	CRUCIFIX	A cross with the form of Jesus on it
8.	DECEPTIVE	Misleading; to make others believe something that is not true
9.	DESTITUTE	Lacking food, clothing, and shelter
10.	DICTATES	Guiding principles
11.	DIVINE	Supremely good or beautiful; magnificent
12.	ENDURE	Carry on despite hardships
13.	ENTWINED	Around or twisted together
14.	FIERCE	Furiously intense; wild; violent in force
15.	GALOSHES	Waterproof boot or shoe
16.	GANGLING	Awkwardly tall or long-limbed
17.	GRIEVES	Feels sorrow or distress
18.	GRUMBLE	Muttering a complaint
19.	IMPOSING	Very impressive because of great size, stately appearance, or dignity
20.	INCITING	Stirring up, encouraging or prompting into action
21.	INORDINATE	Exceeding reasonable limits; uncontrolled
22.	LUNATIC	Insane person
23.	LYNCHED	Hanged, as by a mob, without due process of the law
24.	MEEK	Tame; gentle; kind
25.	NEUTRAL	Belonging to neither side in a controversy
26.	PEERED	Looked intently, searchingly, or with difficulty
27.	PERDITION	Future state of the wicked; damnation; hell
28.	PERSECUTION	Punishment or harassment usually of a severe nature on the basis of race, religion, or political opinion
29.	PETITION	Formal request
30.	PINNACLE	The highest point, as with success, power, or fame
31.	RAIDING	Conducting a surprise attack on another's property with the purpose of taking goods
32.	RATTLED	Flustered; unnerved; confused
33.	REIGN	Rule or hold authority; dominate with power or influence
34.	RUBBISH	Nonsense; worthless material; garbage
35.	RUSTIC	Typical of country life of country people

No.	Word	Clue/Definition
36.	SANATORIUM	Institution for the treatment of certain chronic diseases or various nervous or mental disorders
37.	SCOLD	Reprimand or criticize harshly and usually angrily
38.	SENSIBLY	Showing good sense or sound judgment
39.	SPECTACLES	Eyeglasses
40.	STAMPEDE	Frenzied rush of a mass of people
41.	STOUT	Firm; strong; having endurance
42.	STRIFE	Conflict; struggle; clash
43.	STRUTTED	Walked in a pompous way
44.	UNSCRUPULOUS	Without principles
45.	URGING	Encouraging
46.	VEXED	Irritated; annoyed
47.	VIGILANT	On the alert; watchful
48.	WIELD	Exercise power, or influence as in ruling or dominating
49.	WRINGING	Extracting or expelling by twisting or compression

VOCABULARY WORD SEARCH Witness

S A N A T O R I U M D E C E P T I V E D
C D X M L I N O R D I N A T E P Y W N R
X R I H Y J M G G I C G Y U L E S V T M
L J U C Z Z F K N O M M S T R T E E W S
W P G C T P Q H N Y N P R I F I V N I D
Y H Q S I A N S D L E R O T N T E D N K
R Q R D T F T V S Q U M Z S J I I U E S
Y S X H D A I E X T T R T E I O R R D Y
G R U M B L E X S D R A I D I N G E H E
D X E L P R L E E D A I E B G F G S N M
L E E T F B I D N D L L F I B T I I G R
K Y T S M I N G E D T W E E Q B V S A R
S P N D T A E T A T N R R N B I P E N Z
T P H C R O C R A D S I U U D I I N G S
A M E B H U U R C S E N R S W N N S L Z
M W P E D E N T D E U G L T T C N I I P
P Y I N R N D L P H R I U R J I A B N J
E T O E Q E O S Q S G N N U T T C L G W
D C M X L C D L W O I G A T B I L Y J G
E D H S S D T P Z L N V T T H N E B P L
C L E R G Y M A N A G X I E B G V S G H
S H B Q T N A L I G I V C D J K F W F C

BRANDED	DIVINE	INCITING	RAIDING	STOUT
BRIGADE	ENDURE	INORDINATE	RATTLED	STRIFE
CLERGYMAN	ENTWINED	LUNATIC	REIGN	STRUTTED
CONDUCTED	FIERCE	LYNCHED	RUBBISH	URGING
CONSTABLE	GALOSHES	MEEK	RUSTIC	VEXED
CRUCIFIX	GANGLING	NEUTRAL	SANATORIUM	VIGILANT
DECEPTIVE	GRIEVES	PEERED	SCOLD	WIELD
DESTITUTE	GRUMBLE	PETITION	SENSIBLY	WRINGING
DICTATES	IMPOSING	PINNACLE	STAMPEDE	

VOCABULARY WORD SEARCH Witness

S	A	N	A	T	O	R	I	U	M	D	E	C	E	P	T	I	V	E	
C	D				I	N	O	R	D	I	N	A	T	E	P			N	
	R	I							I	C			U		E	S		T	
		U	C						O	M			T		T	E	E	W	
			C	T				N		N	P		I		I	V	N	I	
				I	A		S			E		O	T		T	E	D	N	
					F	T	V	S		U			S		I	I	U	E	
					A	I	E		T	T			E	I	O	R	R	D	
G	R	U	M	B	L	E	X	S	D	R	A	I	D	I	N	G	E	H	E
		E	L		R		E	E			A	E		G		G	S	N	
L	E	E		F		I	D		D	L	L	F	I			I	I	G	
K	Y		S		I	N	G	E		T	W	E	E		B	V	S	A	
S		N		T	A	E	T	A	T		R			B	I	P	E	N	
T	P		C	R	O	C	R	A	D		I	U	U	D	I	I	N	G	
A		E	B	H	U	U	R	C	S	E	N	R	S		N	N	S	L	
M	W		E	D	E		T	D	E	U	G	L	T	T	C	N	I	I	
P		I	N	R		D	L		H	R	I	U	R		I	A	B	N	
E		O	E		E	O			S	G	N	N	U		T	C	L	G	
D	C			L	C	D			O	I	G	A	T		I	L	Y		
E				S	D				L	N		T	T		N	E			
C	L	E	R	G	Y	M	A	N	A	G		I	E		G				
				T	N	A	L	I	G	I	V	C	D						

BRANDED	DIVINE	INCITING	RAIDING	STOUT
BRIGADE	ENDURE	INORDINATE	RATTLED	STRIFE
CLERGYMAN	ENTWINED	LUNATIC	REIGN	STRUTTED
CONDUCTED	FIERCE	LYNCHED	RUBBISH	URGING
CONSTABLE	GALOSHES	MEEK	RUSTIC	VEXED
CRUCIFIX	GANGLING	NEUTRAL	SANATORIUM	VIGILANT
DECEPTIVE	GRIEVES	PEERED	SCOLD	WIELD
DESTITUTE	GRUMBLE	PETITION	SENSIBLY	WRINGING
DICTATES	IMPOSING	PINNACLE	STAMPEDE	

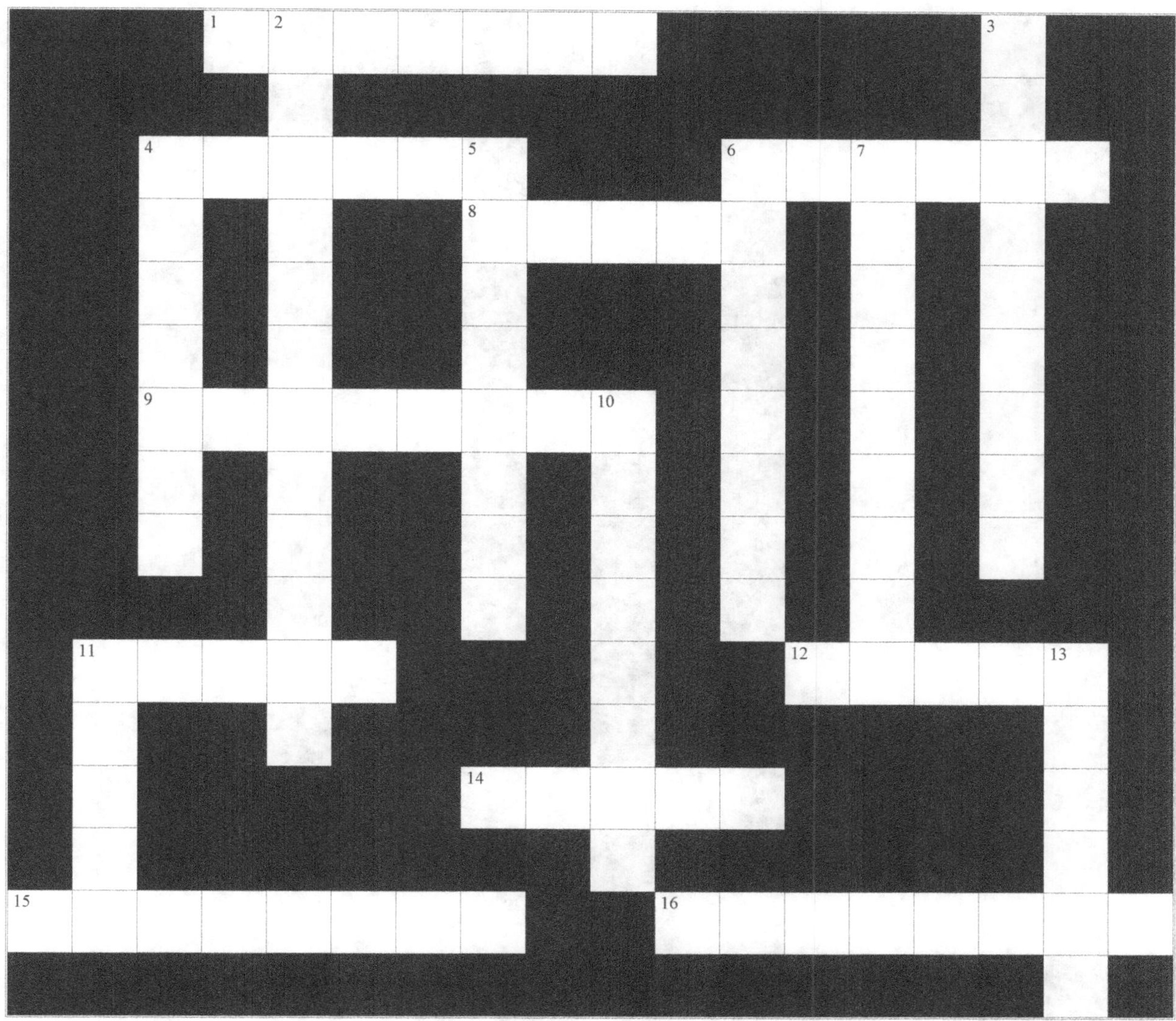

Across

1. Nonsense; worthless material; garbage
4. Typical of country life of country people
6. Carry on despite hardships
8. Rule or hold authority; dominate with power or influence
9. Very impressive because of great size, stately appearance, or dignity
11. Firm; strong; having endurance
12. Irritated; annoyed
14. Exercise power, or influence as in ruling or dominating
15. Recommending; suggesting
16. Extracting or expelling by twisting or compression

Down

2. Without principles
3. Future state of the wicked; damnation; hell
4. Conducting a surprise attack on another's property with the purpose of taking goods
5. A cross with the form of Jesus on it
6. Around or twisted together
7. Misleading; to make others believe something that is not true
10. Waterproof boot or shoe
11. Reprimand or criticize harshly and usually angrily
13. Supremely good or beautiful; magnificent

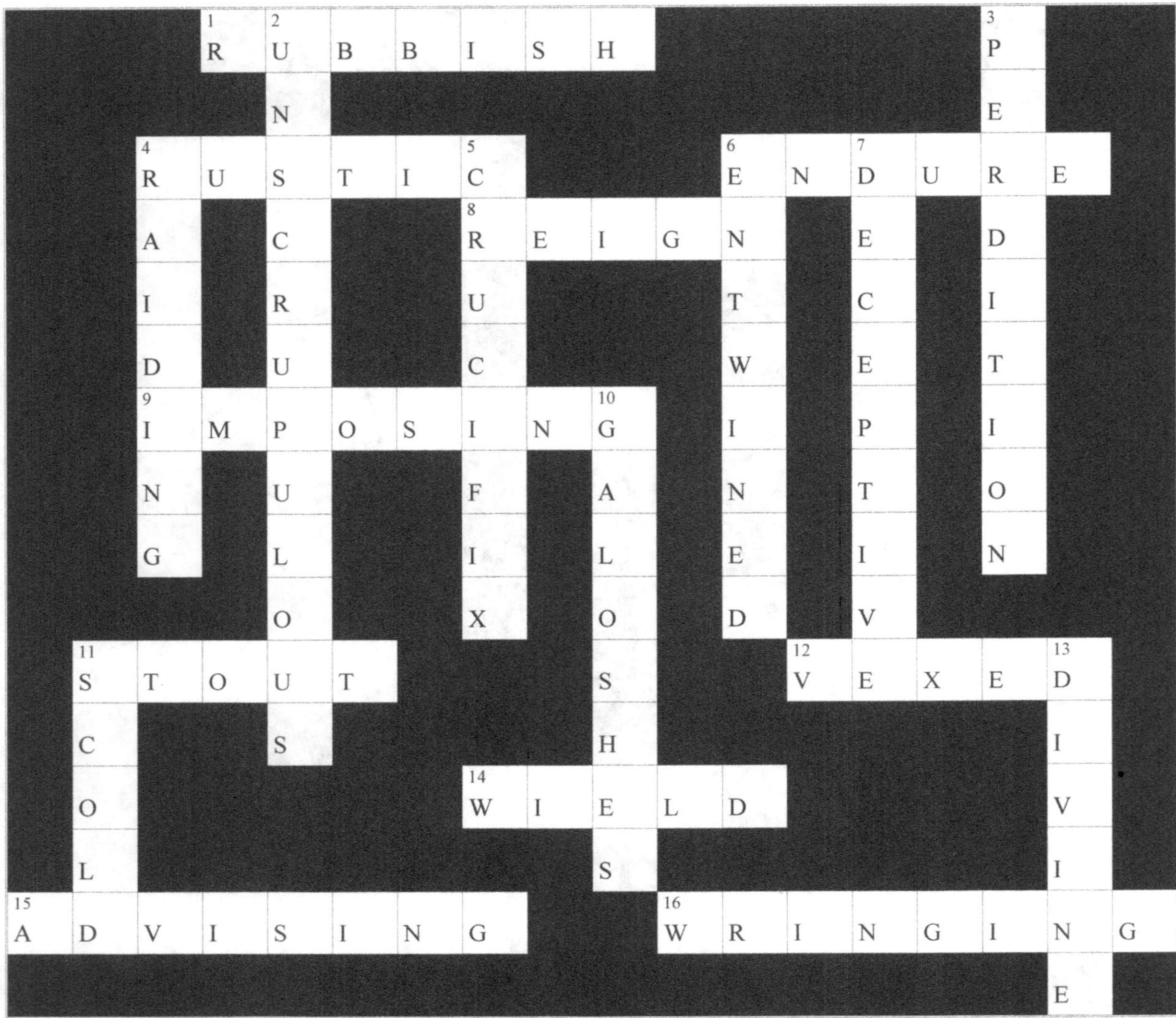

Across
1. Nonsense; worthless material; garbage
4. Typical of country life of country people
6. Carry on despite hardships
8. Rule or hold authority; dominate with power or influence
9. Very impressive because of great size, stately appearance, or dignity
11. Firm; strong; having endurance
12. Irritated; annoyed
14. Exercise power, or influence as in ruling or dominating
15. Recommending; suggesting
16. Extracting or expelling by twisting or compression

Down
2. Without principles
3. Future state of the wicked; damnation; hell
4. Conducting a surprise attack on another's property with the purpose of taking goods
5. A cross with the form of Jesus on it
6. Around or twisted together
7. Misleading; to make others believe something that is not true
10. Waterproof boot or shoe
11. Reprimand or criticize harshly and usually angrily
13. Supremely good or beautiful; magnificent

VOCABULARY MATCHING 1 *Witness*

____ 1.	BRIGADE	A.	Lacking food, clothing, and shelter
____ 2.	PERDITION	B.	Waterproof boot or shoe
____ 3.	PERSECUTION	C.	The highest point, as with success, power, or fame
____ 4.	PINNACLE	D.	Rule or hold authority; dominate with power or influence
____ 5.	REIGN	E.	Insane person
____ 6.	SANATORIUM	F.	Awkwardly tall or long-limbed
____ 7.	SPECTACLES	G.	Punishment or harassment usually of a severe nature on the basis of race, religion, or political opinion
____ 8.	STRIFE	H.	Exceeding reasonable limits; uncontrolled
____ 9.	URGING	I.	Conflict; struggle; clash
____ 10.	MEEK	J.	Eyeglasses
____ 11.	LUNATIC	K.	Peace officer with less authority than a sheriff
____ 12.	CONSTABLE	L.	Tame; gentle; kind
____ 13.	DECEPTIVE	M.	Institution for the treatment of certain chronic diseases or various nervous or mental disorders
____ 14.	DESTITUTE	N.	Muttering a complaint
____ 15.	ENDURE	O.	Large body of troops; a military unit
____ 16.	GALOSHES	P.	Future state of the wicked; damnation; hell
____ 17.	GANGLING	Q.	Encouraging
____ 18.	GRUMBLE	R.	Carry on despite hardships
____ 19.	INORDINATE	S.	Misleading; to make others believe something that is not true
____ 20.	WIELD	T.	Exercise power, or influence as in ruling or dominating

VOCABULARY MATCHING 1 ANSWER KEY *Witness*

Answer	No.	Word	Definition
O	1.	BRIGADE	A. Lacking food, clothing, and shelter
P	2.	PERDITION	B. Waterproof boot or shoe
G	3.	PERSECUTION	C. The highest point, as with success, power, or fame
C	4.	PINNACLE	D. Rule or hold authority; dominate with power or influence
D	5.	REIGN	E. Insane person
M	6.	SANATORIUM	F. Awkwardly tall or long-limbed
J	7.	SPECTACLES	G. Punishment or harassment usually of a severe nature on the basis of race, religion, or political opinion
I	8.	STRIFE	H. Exceeding reasonable limits; uncontrolled
Q	9.	URGING	I. Conflict; struggle; clash
L	10.	MEEK	J. Eyeglasses
E	11.	LUNATIC	K. Peace officer with less authority than a sheriff
K	12.	CONSTABLE	L. Tame; gentle; kind
S	13.	DECEPTIVE	M. Institution for the treatment of certain chronic diseases or various nervous or mental disorders
A	14.	DESTITUTE	N. Muttering a complaint
R	15.	ENDURE	O. Large body of troops; a military unit
B	16.	GALOSHES	P. Future state of the wicked; damnation; hell
F	17.	GANGLING	Q. Encouraging
N	18.	GRUMBLE	R. Carry on despite hardships
H	19.	INORDINATE	S. Misleading; to make others believe something that is not true
T	20.	WIELD	T. Exercise power, or influence as in ruling or dominating

VOCABULARY MATCHING 2 *Witness*

____ 1. ADVISING	A.	On the alert; watchful
____ 2. RAIDING	B.	Christian minister
____ 3. RUSTIC	C.	Recommending; suggesting
____ 4. SCOLD	D.	Tame; gentle; kind
____ 5. STAMPEDE	E.	Without principles
____ 6. STRIFE	F.	Conflict; struggle; clash
____ 7. UNSCRUPULOUS	G.	Typical of country life of country people
____ 8. VEXED	H.	Exercise power, or influence as in ruling or dominating
____ 9. VIGILANT	I.	Around or twisted together
____ 10. PETITION	J.	Awkwardly tall or long-limbed
____ 11. PERDITION	K.	Future state of the wicked; damnation; hell
____ 12. CLERGYMAN	L.	A cross with the form of Jesus on it
____ 13. CRUCIFIX	M.	Very impressive because of great size, stately appearance, or dignity
____ 14. DICTATES	N.	Formal request
____ 15. ENTWINED	O.	Conducting a surprise attack on another's property with the purpose of taking goods
____ 16. GANGLING	P.	Stirring up, encouraging or prompting into action
____ 17. IMPOSING	Q.	Reprimand or criticize harshly and usually angrily
____ 18. INCITING	R.	Irritated; annoyed
____ 19. MEEK	S.	Frenzied rush of a mass of people
____ 20. WIELD	T.	Guiding principles

VOCABULARY MATCHING 2 ANSWER KEY *Witness*

C	1. ADVISING	A. On the alert; watchful
O	2. RAIDING	B. Christian minister
G	3. RUSTIC	C. Recommending; suggesting
Q	4. SCOLD	D. Tame; gentle; kind
S	5. STAMPEDE	E. Without principles
F	6. STRIFE	F. Conflict; struggle; clash
E	7. UNSCRUPULOUS	G. Typical of country life of country people
R	8. VEXED	H. Exercise power, or influence as in ruling or dominating
A	9. VIGILANT	I. Around or twisted together
N	10. PETITION	J. Awkwardly tall or long-limbed
K	11. PERDITION	K. Future state of the wicked; damnation; hell
B	12. CLERGYMAN	L. A cross with the form of Jesus on it
L	13. CRUCIFIX	M. Very impressive because of great size, stately appearance, or dignity
T	14. DICTATES	N. Formal request
I	15. ENTWINED	O. Conducting a surprise attack on another's property with the purpose of taking goods
J	16. GANGLING	P. Stirring up, encouraging or prompting into action
M	17. IMPOSING	Q. Reprimand or criticize harshly and usually angrily
P	18. INCITING	R. Irritated; annoyed
D	19. MEEK	S. Frenzied rush of a mass of people
H	20. WIELD	T. Guiding principles

VOCABULARY JUGGLE LETTER 1 *Witness*

______________ = 1. RUAOSATNIM
Institution for the treatment of certain chronic diseases or various nervous or mental disorders

______________ = 2. VLGTINIA
On the alert; watchful

______________ = 3. OULUPNUSRSUC
Without principles

______________ = 4. CAELESSTPC
Eyeglasses

______________ = 5. AERBDDN
Symbol burned on with a hot iron

______________ = 6. NGLCERAMY
Christian minister

______________ = 7. TEPECIDEV
Misleading; to make others believe something that is not true

______________ = 8. NNTIEWED
Around or twisted together

______________ = 9. ASHLOGES
Waterproof boot or shoe

______________ = 10. NIGALGGN
Awkwardly tall or long-limbed

______________ = 11. ULMEBRG
Muttering a complaint

______________ = 12. INNICTGI
Stirring up, encouraging or prompting into action

______________ = 13. AUNLCIT
Insane person

______________ = 14. MEKE
Tame; gentle; kind

______________ = 15. ROUEEPNISTC
Punishment or harassment usually of a severe nature on the basis of race, religion, or political opinion

______________ = 16. NNILECPA
The highest point, as with success, power, or fame

______________ = 17. BRBUIHS
Nonsense; worthless material; garbage

______________ = 18. WGNIRGIN
Extracting or expelling by twisting or compression

VOCABULARY JUGGLE LETTER 1 ANSWER KEY *Witness*

SANATORIUM	= 1.	RUAOSATNIM Institution for the treatment of certain chronic diseases or various nervous or mental disorders
VIGILANT	= 2.	VLGTINIA On the alert; watchful
UNSCRUPULOUS	= 3.	OULUPNUSRSUC Without principles
SPECTACLES	= 4.	CAELESSTPC Eyeglasses
BRANDED	= 5.	AERBDDN Symbol burned on with a hot iron
CLERGYMAN	= 6.	NGLCERAMY Christian minister
DECEPTIVE	= 7.	TEPECIDEV Misleading; to make others believe something that is not true
ENTWINED	= 8.	NNTIEWED Around or twisted together
GALOSHES	= 9.	ASHLOGES Waterproof boot or shoe
GANGLING	= 10.	NIGALGGN Awkwardly tall or long-limbed
GRUMBLE	= 11.	ULMEBRG Muttering a complaint
INCITING	= 12.	INNICTGI Stirring up, encouraging or prompting into action
LUNATIC	= 13.	AUNLCIT Insane person
MEEK	= 14.	MEKE Tame; gentle; kind
PERSECUTION	= 15.	ROUEEPNISTC Punishment or harassment usually of a severe nature on the basis of race, religion, or political opinion
PINNACLE	= 16.	NNILECPA The highest point, as with success, power, or fame
RUBBISH	= 17.	BRBUIHS Nonsense; worthless material; garbage
WRINGING	= 18.	WGNIRGIN Extracting or expelling by twisting or compression

VOCABULARY JUGGLE LETTER 2 *Witness*

_______________ = 1. SPEEDMAT
Frenzied rush of a mass of people

_______________ = 2. RUGGIN
Encouraging

_______________ = 3. URTTESTD
Walked in a pompous way

_______________ = 4. IFRSTE
Conflict; struggle; clash

_______________ = 5. NIDAIVGS
Recommending; suggesting

_______________ = 6. BEDGRAI
Large body of troops; a military unit

_______________ = 7. DCCTDOENU
The way a person acts, especially from the standpoint of morality and ethics

_______________ = 8. CSANELTOB
Peace officer with less authority than a sheriff

_______________ = 9. RIIFCXUC
A cross with the form of Jesus on it

_______________ = 10. UTEETDITS
Lacking food, clothing, and shelter

_______________ = 11. ERIVEGS
Feels sorrow or distress

_______________ = 12. EIOTNNARID
Exceeding reasonable limits; uncontrolled

_______________ = 13. NAERTLU
Belonging to neither side in a controversy

_______________ = 14. INTDRPOIE
Future state of the wicked; damnation; hell

_______________ = 15. ATRTDEL
Flustered; unnerved; confused

_______________ = 16. IRENG
Rule or hold authority; dominate with power or influence

_______________ = 17. UTICRS
Typical of country life of country people

_______________ = 18. EVDEX
Irritated; annoyed

VOCABULARY JUGGLE LETTER 2 ANSWER KEY *Witness*

STAMPEDE	= 1.	SPEEDMAT Frenzied rush of a mass of people
URGING	= 2.	RUGGIN Encouraging
STRUTTED	= 3.	URTTESTD Walked in a pompous way
STRIFE	= 4.	IFRSTE Conflict; struggle; clash
ADVISING	= 5.	NIDAIVGS Recommending; suggesting
BRIGADE	= 6.	BEDGRAI Large body of troops; a military unit
CONDUCTED	= 7.	DCCTDOENU The way a person acts, especially from the standpoint of morality and ethics
CONSTABLE	= 8.	CSANELTOB Peace officer with less authority than a sheriff
CRUCIFIX	= 9.	RIIFCXUC A cross with the form of Jesus on it
DESTITUTE	= 10.	UTEETDITS Lacking food, clothing, and shelter
GRIEVES	= 11.	ERIVEGS Feels sorrow or distress
INORDINATE	= 12.	EIOTNNARID Exceeding reasonable limits; uncontrolled
NEUTRAL	= 13.	NAERTLU Belonging to neither side in a controversy
PERDITION	= 14.	INTDRPOIE Future state of the wicked; damnation; hell
RATTLED	= 15.	ATRTDEL Flustered; unnerved; confused
REIGN	= 16.	IRENG Rule or hold authority; dominate with power or influence
RUSTIC	= 17.	UTICRS Typical of country life of country people
VEXED	= 18.	EVDEX Irritated; annoyed

www.ingramcontent.com/pod-product-compliance
Lightning Source LLC
Chambersburg PA
CBHW082101090726
47910CB00008B/2555

* 9 7 8 1 6 0 2 4 9 4 7 0 1 *